Hsing Yun's Hundred Sayings Series

Keeping Busy Is the Best Nourishment

By Venerable Master Hsing Yun

忙就是營養

Keeping Busy Is the Best Nourishment

Hsing Yun's Hundred Sayings Series 5

Copyright 2002 Venerable Master Hsing Yun

First Published in 2002

Reprinted in Nov. 2002

Foguang Cultural Enterprise Co.,Ltd.

6F, 117 Sec.3,San He Rd., Sanchung,Taipei County,
Taiwan, R.O.C.

ISBN 957-457-068-1

Printed in Taiwan, Republic of China

CONTENTS

Venerable Master Hsing Yun

Founder of Fo Guang Shan

Venerable Master Hsing Yun was born in Chiangsu province, China in 1927. Ordained under Venerable Master Chih Kai at the age of twelve, he became an elite at various Buddhist institutions such as Chi-hsia Vinaya College and Chiao-shan Buddhist College throughout his following twelve years as a student of the Dharma.

Master Hsing Yun arrived in Taiwan in 1949, and soon became the chief editor of the publication of "Life," "Buddhism Today," "Awakening the World" and other magazines. His effort in establishing "Buddhist Chanting Groups," "Buddhist Student Association," "Young Buddhist Association," "Sunday Children's School," "Dharma Promoters' Team," and various libraries in many parts of Taiwan ensured a strong foundation for his subsequent endeavour in the promotion of Dharma.

In 1957, he began to organize the "Buddhist Culture Service Center," the publication of "Buddhism Series" in Chinese and English, various Chinese Sutras in the vernacular style of writing, and audio-visual materials on Buddhism. Each of these projects later became part of the Fo Guang Publishing House which continued to work on the re-compilation of over 300 volumes of "Fo Guang Tripitaka," the 132-volume "Chinese Buddhist Sutras Series," and the eight-volume Fo Guang Buddhist Dictionary.

Master Hsing Yun's grand view of globalization has bridged the gap between Taiwan and many nations. He founded Fo Guang Shan Monastery in 1967, whose main goal is to promote Humanistic Buddhism while abiding by the objectives: "To foster talent through education; to promote Buddhism through culture; to benefit society through charitable programs; to purify human minds through Buddhist practice." Over two hundred branch temples were established in major cities around the world within a short period of only 35 years. Some branches are: Hsi Lai Temple near Los Angeles, Chung Mei Temple in Houston, Fo Guang Shan Temple in Toronto, Nan Tien Temple in Sydney, Chung Tien Temple in Brisbane, I.B.P.S. Holland, Nan Hua Temple in South Africa, etc. Each of the temples mentioned above can accommodate as many as one thousand people for Dharma functions and other activities. At the same time, over fifty Chinese Schools, nine museums, twenty libraries, twelve bookstores and sixteen Buddhist Colleges were established in Taiwan, India, Hong Kong, Malaysia, and Australia. In addition , Chi-Kuang High School, Pu-Men High School, Hsi Lai University in the U. S., Fo Guang University in Ilan, Taiwan, and Nan Hua University in Chiayi, Taiwan, were established as a result of the Master's great resolve.

Master Hsing Yun has achieved all of the above in a systematic and organized manner, making every effort to benefit not himself but others. He also established the "Da Tzu Children's Home," "Fo Guang Senior Home," "Compassion Foundation," "Evergreen House," "Lanyang Home of Love," and other nursing homes and children's homes. Master hopes to offer not only materialistic assistance but spiritual guidance, comfort, and mind purification to all stages of one's life.

To achieve equality between the monastic and laity and to promote Buddhism through combined effort and resources from both, Master Hsing Yun established the Buddha's Light International Association (BLIA) in 1991, followed by BLIA, R.O.C. Headquarters in Taiwan. As the biggest Chinese association in the world, the BLIA now consists of over 173 chapters and 2000 sub-chapters.

For the past ten years, the BLIA has subsequently

held its annual General Conference in the Performing Arts Center of Los Angeles, Fo Guang Shan Taiwan, the Peace Memorial Hall at the University of British Columbia in Canada, the Darling Harbour Convention Center in Sydney, Australia, Le Palais des Congrès in Paris, France, the Hong Kong Coliseum, the Regal Constellation Hotel at Toronto, Canada, and the Chiang Kai-shek Stadium in Taiwan, etc. The number of participants for each of these conferences always exceeds 5,000. The keynote speech given by the Master is the most anticipated program of each year's conference. Topics from past conferences include: "Joy and Harmony," "Oneness and Coexistence," "Respect and Tolerance," "Equality and Peace," "Wholeness and Freeness," "Nature and Life," "One Truth for All," and "Resolve and Development." Each of these topics were translated in both Chinese and English for the audience. Not only do the keynote speeches offer a future direction and spiritual guidance for the BLIA members, the profound message of world peace and human well-being that lies behind each of them have also become a major trend of school in the world

Master Hsing Yun spends his life promoting the concepts of respect, tolerance and harmony. For this purpose, he travels the world and actively participates in religious exchange. Some international conferences organized under his leadership include the World Tantric and Sutric Conference, International Sangha Seminar, International Buddhist Youth Conference, and the International Buddhist Womens Conference. He has also exchanged Women's thoughts, and met with many religious and world leaders such as Ven. Dr. K Sri Dharmananda – Maha Nayaka Thera, Pope John Paul II, the Dalai Lama, the Prime Minister of Malaysia – Mahathir Mohamad, and representatives from Taoist, Christian, Catholic as well as other religious organizations. By crossing the boundaries of religion, sect, and tradition, he brings the world one step closer to world peace and harmony.

In order to restore Bhiksuni Precepts in the Theravadan tradition, Master Hsing Yun brought the Full Ordination Ceremony to Bodhgaya, India in 1998. Hundreds of Bhiksus and Bhiksunis were conferred Full Monastic Precepts in front of elder monks from around the world.

Although Buddhism in China enjoys a history of over 2000 years, the Buddha's Birthday Celebration has never received much attention from the government of Taiwan. By gathering the influence of Buddhists and renowned Buddhist monks, Master Hsing Yun was able to successfully request the Taiwan government to declare the Buddha's Birthday as a national holiday. In 1998, the Master also brought the Buddha's tooth relic from India to Taiwan.

His concern for racial equality inspired many native South Africans to become students of Nan Hua Buddhist Seminary in South Africa. The Buddhist College (Ts'ung Lin University) in Fo Guang Shan, Kaohsiung also accepts students from countries such as Indonesia, Ladakh, the United States, Switzerland, Nepal, and India. He hopes that in twenty year's time, the management of all Fo Guang Shan branch temples around the world can be handed over to natives, so as to actualize his concept of "Localizing Buddhism."

In 1978, Master Hsing Yun was conferred Honorary Doctorate by the University of Oriental Studies. Later on, he received invitations to be the head of the department of Indian Studies at Chinese Culture University, and was a guest professor at Tunghai University. He was also a guest speaker at various universities in the US such as: Yale, Harvard, Massachusetts Institute of Technology, University of California, Cornell, and University of Hawaii; as well as the National University of Singapore, the Ngee Ann Polytechnic University in Singapore, the Bond University in Australia, the Chinese University of Hong Kong, and Hong Kong Polytechnic University. In 1989, he became the first Buddhist monk in history to be invited by a communist country for a public lecture at the Peking University.

Master Hsing Yun's great enthusiasm and deep passion for education and culture are expressed in many ways. The Merit Times newspaper initially established by him in Taiwan is now printed in the United States, this helps create new opportunities for the development of Buddhism. The Buddha's Light Television Network does not show any advertisements and focuses completely on mind purifying programs. Together with Merit Times, they become two streams of purity in today's media. The Master has also united scholars from China and Taiwan to publish the Universal Gate Buddhist Journal. With the assistance from professors in the Peking University, the Szechwan University, the Renmin (People) University and the Nanjing University, the 100-volume "Chinese Buddhist academic Series" was published. This collection of Chinese Dharma library contains Masters' and theses Ph. D. dissertations from both Taiwan and China of the past century. The 100-volume "A Collection of Chinese Buddhist Cultural Essays" will also be published in the near future.

Various foundations have been established since 1988. For example, the "Fo Guang Shan Foundation for Culture and Education," "Fo Guang Pureland Cultural and Educational Foundation," and the "Humanistic Culture and Education Foundation." These foundations are responsible for organizing all kinds of international academic seminars and conferences as well as the publication of related journals. Furthermore, the World Buddhist Examination provided a different type of learning experience for all walks of life. From the illiterate elderly to preschool children, students to professors, convicts to laborers, pop stars to members of parliament, and from Taiwan to other nations, the total number of candidates taking the exam once reached two million. Though called an examination, this event created a fresh atmosphere for developing the habit of reading which can strengthen people's ability to differentiate the right from the wrong.

As the president of the Buddha's Light International Association, the Master has organized various conferences for men, women and young adults on a regular basis. The Annual Children's Happy Camp at Fo Guang Shan, Kaohsiung has always attracted thousands of children. Other events such as "Compassion and Love Campaign," "Three Acts of Goodness," and "The Seven Admonitions" continue to radiate their influence on the purification of human minds and society, and bring endless benefit to people's lives. The Fo Guang Shan Buddhist Hymn Choir has followed Master Hsing Yun's footsteps to Hong Kong, the United States, Canada, Australia, England, France, and Germany. The Sydney Opera House and New York's Lincoln Center, in particular, were two of the choir's major stops when their performance received a standing ovation and much positive response. No doubt, this is yet another example of cultural exchange.

Master Hsing Yun has set his footsteps on many parts of the world including Russia, Germany, America, Egypt, South Africa, New Zealand, Australia, Singapore and Malaysia. He has also brought Buddhism into jails, factories, industrial enterprises, schools, remote areas and even Vietnamese refugee camps in Hong Kong. Being an excellent speaker, his Dharma talks and lectures have attracted millions of listeners through these years. While actively promoting Buddhism, his passion for literature and writing have resulted in the publication of more than 70 books for readership ranging from the general public to the academic circle. Many of which have won awards for excellent reading material from the Board of Education in Taiwan or recognized as set text for members from the Ministry of National Defense in Taiwan. His works have been translated into English, Japanese, German, French, Korean, Portuguese, Sinhalese, Spanish and Thai for circulation around the world. Some have even become best sellers in certain countries.

Equal emphasis is placed on charitable activities, Fo Guang Shan adopted nine primary schools in the Taiwan Earthquake in 1999, three of which must be constructed from the beginning and six required partly reconstruction. While offering material assistance, spiritual consultation is also provided to the victims of the earthquake. Fo Guang Yuan stations were set up throughout the affected area and their services are still continuing to the present. Master Hsing Yun also traveled as far as Honduras, Costa Rica, Papua New Guinea, Ladakh, and the Philippines to conduct emergency relief programs. His contribution to international exchange and world peace is truly admirable!

Master Hsing Yun has won many awards for Foreign Relations, Education, Culture, Charity and Social Education from the government of Taiwan. For example, in May 1997, he was awarded first grade medal of excellence from the Ministry of the Interior and the Ministry of Foreign Affairs, making him the first Buddhist monk in history to receive this honor. Two years later, he was awarded a second National Civic Service Award, signifying the government's recognition for his contribution to the nation, society, and Buddhism. In 1978, he became the first citizen of Taiwan to be conferred Honorary Doctorate by the University of Oriental Studies. In 1995, he was awarded the Buddha Ratna Award at the All India Buddhist Conference. Thailand's Prime Minister Chuan Leekpai awarded him a "Merit Medal for Great Contribution to Buddhism" at the 21st WFB General Conference in 2001. California and Houston have also conferred him Honorary Citizenship, once again proving Master's reputation around the world. Master Hsing Yun has also been invited to conduct various religious ceremonies by the United States government.

"The essence of Buddhism is peace!" To spread the seeds of peace, Master Hsing Yun brought the 16th World Fellowship of Buddhists Conference to Hsi Lai Temple in Los Angeles, making it the first time in history for a WFB conference to be held outside Asia. What made this conference even more significant was the fact that delegates from China and Taiwan were brought to the same meeting table, breaking the barrier between the two shores and realizing the annual theme "WFB Unity for World Peace." Subsequently, the Master organized two more WFB General Conferences in Fo Guang Shan Taiwan, and Nan Tien Temple in Australia. Master's organizing ability received such recognition and praise from members of the WFB, who unanimously agreed for him to be WFB Honorary President. Master Hsing Yun became the first Chinese in history to receive this honour.

Master Hsing Yun has enabled Buddhism to develop in a systematic, modern, humanistic, and global manner. His achievement and merit are truly magnificent. Just as Mr. Zhao Puchu, the former President of the Buddhist Association of China said, "What the Buddha could not achieve in history is all done by Master Hsing Yun now!" However, as the Master feels indifferent to fame or gain, even his disciples are unaware of everything he has ever done. One of the visible traces we can use to Master's achievements is through his poetry, "A mind with the compassionate resolve to liberate all beings; A body that is like an untied boat drifting in the vast ocean of Dharma; If you shall ask what I have done all my life. The Buddha's Light has shone on the World!" His compassion and grand resolve is a blessing for world peace and human well-being. Indeed, Master Hsing Yun is one of the most admired and respected religious leaders of today.

INTRODUCTION

As I read the stimulating essays in Venerable Grand Master Hsing Yun's latest book in English, *Keeping Busy Is the Best Nourishment,* a verse I had learned in primary school in the central hills of Sri Lanka came to my mind:

> *Lives of great men all remind us*
> *We can make our lives sublime*
> *And, departing, leave behind us*
> *Footprints on the sands of time.*

The last line of H.W. Longfellow's verse has long been my criterion of the true greatness of a man or woman. How well this criterion applies to the Grand Master! Enormous in number and intrinsic significance are the indelible, giant footprints, which the Grand Master Hsing Yun has imprinted on the sands of time. Fo Guang Shan Buddhist Order and its many religious and educational institutions spanning the continents of Asia, America, Australia, and Africa are lasting edifices to his indefatigable energy to promote the wisdom of Buddhism in the modern world. Far more durable are his insights and convictions, thoughts and reflections which are permanently preserved in his manifold publications. He is thus a creator of living history.

This volume which I have the honor of introducing to readers is another footprint on the sands of time. This description becomes very apt when it is observed that every chapter spans time and space without any boundaries. Each chapter heading is an aphorism which concisely summarizes numerous experiences of the Grand Master's life. Thus "*A Job Without Pay*" is a eulogy on voluntary work and the illustrations come from his own life and those of his close associates.

"In doing '*A Job Without Pay,*' there is dignity, sincerity of dedication, joy of aspiration, and endless worth," he says. He adds further, "It is fun to do '*A Job Without Pay.*' Throughout my life, I have never had a summer or winter vacation, a weekend off, New Year holidays, or any other holiday, and I have never demanded any special privilege. I never got my salary when I was the principal of the White Tower Elementary School in China. I told my Dharma brother, 'Please divide my salary into two parts, one for the temple and the other for my mother." Out of his experience, he draws the conclusion 'Having is finite and exhaustible, but not-having is infinite and inexhaustible.'

"*Don't be a Dolphin*" begins with the image of a performing dolphin at Sea World that gets a small fish as reward for its efforts. The Grand Master would compare a disciple fishing for a reward or praise after finishing a job to such a dolphin. Arguing logically through years of his own life experiences, he urges us to "embrace the ideal of benefiting society without a thought of reward." He aimed at getting metaphorically a big fish.

He says, "I established Hsi Lai University in Los Angeles to facilitate a cultural exchange between East and West, and I hope I have contributed to humanistic thinking there. Isn't that getting a big fish in return?"

Out of an inspiring discussion which covers Buddhist history of China and the Grand Master's own eventful life, he concludes,

*"Merit with attachment is finite and limited, while the merit of non-attachment is infinite and limitless."

*"The great practice and cultivation show us that only when we get along and handle affairs without asking anything in return are we respected

and successful."

*"We need to understand that the meaning of life is to enlarge life continually in the universe. To lead an energetic life, we need to have a great vision and not perform for small fish."

Chapter after chapter opens new vistas of practical guidelines to an enlightened life style. With hardly a direct reference, the principles and practices of humanistic Buddhism are elaborated and illustrated with interesting anecdotes. These anecdotes are drawn from life experiences of scholars and sages, emperors and leaders, and humble monks and peasants. The entire spectrum of Chinese civilization of two thousand and more years is covered along with the Grand Master's own experience right up to the time of Chiang Kai-shek. The most touching are the vignettes of his life as the following will show:

"I entered monasticism at twelve and studied at the Buddhist College. Life was hard then. I never had a chance to wear new clothes, just those of the departed. I never had enough food, and ate rice once every two weeks. The broth was clean as water, without oil or vegetable. In the big monastery, it was not unusual to be mistreated. The conservative monastic education included frequent scolding. But my ten years passed quickly. While many monastics quit halfway, I regarded the training "as it should be." I didn't indulge in gossip or "haggle" about the treatment. Consequently, I could learn and practice with a tranquil mind and benefit from the Dharma joy."

The lessons which the Grand Master has derived for our benefit are most timely. "Don't compare and haggle with others," he tells us and illustrates the efficacy of his advice with reference to how he rose above envy and jealousy, handled slander, dealt with criticism even when it was undeserved, and responded to success with humility. He says,

"When I founded Fo Guang Shan, I didn't know that it would be the foundation for over one hundred branch temples and organizations worldwide. On reflection, I realize that I play a role in Buddhism not because of my wisdom or ability, but because my disciples work as a team."

He says further,

"When I lecture around the world, many overseas Chinese ask how I attained my success. I always speak from experience: 'Don't criticize self-interest. Serve the community and do your part, with others, to create a beautiful future.'"

The essay entitled "*Even the Buddha was Slandered*" is a masterpiece of autobiographical reflection of a great being who followed his own advice:

"In this chaotic world of gossip and error, we should leap yet higher and farther, like a balloon in flight, after slanderous attacks."

His most pragmatic advice is supported by statements like the following:

"When I started advocating humanistic Buddhism, many sneered behind my back, or accused me to my face of merely craving attention. Years later, many people now follow our teachings. Scholars in China, Russia, and elsewhere have done research on humanistic Buddhism. We know that people sometimes slander us out of ignorance. We should advance our ideals with words, and prove their value by actions."

In another chapter, the Grand Master presents an in-depth analysis of the Buddhist philosophical concept that "Good causes and conditions lead to success." Again he delves into his life-experience where all causes and conditions have not been always favorable. But he turned them around by dint of his perseverance and his unflinching optimism:

"As for the wars and disasters, poverty and hunger, hardships and difficulties, they became facilitating 'causes and conditions.'"

With equal depth of analysis, he urges us to be busy and occupied:

"It is a fact that my body and mind are healthy because I have been very busy...Keeping busy made me realize how much hard work is needed to produce our worldly goods, and it gave me insight into the essence of dependent origination. That has benefited me all my life."

It is the same message but with a profound philosophical twist when he discusses issues of ultimate concern in the thought-provoking essay, "*There Is Time to Rest Forever.*" What does he wish in life now and in lives to come? He says,

*I hope I am lucky enough to make a grand death by passing away while busy at work.

*Death looks to us like the end of life. But it is not really the end...I vow to be reborn to this saha world as a monk, again and again, to spread the Buddhist teachings and save sentient beings.

I read this new book of Venerable Grand Master Hsing Yun to understand what goes on in his magnificent mind and what drives this human dynamo to incessant activity. Every page has been a revelation. Much have I gathered of the history of Chinese Buddhism and of great persons who inspired him. Even more have I learned from his perspicacious analysis of the unique experience of a life dedicated solely to the good and benefit of others. As usual, the Grand Master leaves you yearning for more -- more of his insights, vision, and wisdom.

Ananda W.P. Guruge
Formerly Ambassador of
Sir Lanka to UNESCO, France, and U.S.A.

PREFACE

I am often asked, "Please give me a sentence I can use as my motto." Always seeking to oblige, I have given out many "sentences" over the years, one at a time. One must avoid the easy temptation to give out the same "one sentence" to everybody. The "sentence" you give must be tailored to the receiver. When the Sixth Patriarch of the Chinese Ch'an school, Hui Neng, was still a simple woodcutter, he gained a degree of enlightenment upon hearing, "One should act without attachment", from the *Diamond Sutra*. Seeking to learn the t'ao (way) from the Fifth Patriarch, Hung Jen, he pounded rice for eight months, until he attained enlightenment and realized his true nature. When Tan Hsia, on his way to the capital for an examination, heard, "Better to cultivate Buddha nature than be appointed an official," he resolved to become a monk in order to learn the Dharma. With diligent practice and cultivation, he became a great Ch'an master.

The *Agama Sutra* says, "Heed good words." Being blessed with a disposition to heed good words, whenever I encounter an apt sentence I engrave it in my memory, to my great advantage. Here are some examples:

An ancient maxim cited by my master, Chih K'ai, "To be outstanding, start with serving others," conveys the sanctity of work and the importance of service.

Venerable Chih Feng's admonition, "Don't become the withered bud or rotten seed of Buddhism," reminds me to keep my Bodhi mind[1] no matter where I go.

Venerable Ch'en Kung's remark, "Buddhism depends on me," compels me to persevere without whining, even in desperate situations.

Venerable Tung Chu's adage, "Only the money you spend wisely is yours to keep," instructs me that wealth should be used to guide the multitude to the treasure of prajna,[2] which is limitless and cannot be depleted.

As a child, I heard my maternal grandmother say, "Deficiency is another form of beauty." And I heard my mother say, "To mediate disputes and resolve conflicts is no trivial matter." I learned "reappraising value" from the great educator Dr. John Dewey, and I observed that the public often

---

[1] The mind to seek enlightenment. It is the seed of the Buddha. One who is initiated in the Bodhi mind and practices diligently will attain enlightenment.
[2] Wisdom.

misses the meaning of "benefiting others". These wise sayings have become my maxims for getting along and handling affairs.

Here are other "sentences" I use when I get along and handle affairs:

"Spread happiness around the world."

"Don't let Amitabha Buddha repay favors for us."

"Make contribution for devotees."

"Be a volunteers' volunteer."

"Muscles must be alive."

"You're important, he's important, I'm not."

"Being moved is most beautiful."

"Keeping busy is the best nourishment."

"Illness is a good medicine."

"The fun of not knowing."

Whenever I use a sentence as the basis of a lecture, it spreads rapidly among my disciples. Such is the power of every "one sentence". It is no wonder that "one sentence" books have spurred many famous people to success. For that reason, *Universal Gate* magazine long ago invited readers to submit short proverbs.

The hope that my shared experiences would empower the multitude to overcome obstacles is now somewhat subdued. I have been warned that, though a sentence may stir the spirit, it is more usual "to have the illusion of enlightenment, but to flop when put to the test." But the collected "one sentence" maxims that mirror the vicissitudes of my life can be a valuable stimulus for the young. Since July 1992, I have narrated my life story in a series of articles, each focused on "one sentence." These were recorded by my disciple Man Guo, a graduate of Fu Jen University and Fo Guang Shan's Buddhist college, to be shared with the public. My earliest articles were published by *Universal Gate* magazine, and afterwards by *Global Views Monthly* and *Better Life Monthly.* In seven years, I wrote one hundred "one sentence" articles, which were published in several books in the *Hsing Yun's Hundred Sayings Series.*

When I began the *Hundred Sayings,* I thought I could produce a hundred articles in ten years by delivering one every month. But what if I should die after finishing just sixty or seventy? How could there be a *Hundred Sayings?* In that case, said some of my disciples, they would finish them for me. After all, it was not unprecedented for disciples to finish what their masters had begun. Happily, I have lived to complete this grand project.

Since publishing *Hsing Yun's Hundred Sayings,* I have most of all delighted in the many readers who have shared with me their Dharma joy.

Some say that when they came to understand "perfectly willing" their job performance improved dramatically.

Some say that after grasping "the rarest of encounters" the world became precious and wonderful.

Some say that "it's important to be brave" nourishes their confidence and perseverance in difficult situations.

Some say that "keeping busy is the best nourishment" gives their work renewed vigor.

My readers are transformed by the sentences because, after grasping their essence, they apply them to their daily lives. The maxims in *Hsing Yun's Hundred Sayings* cannot be realized by the discriminating mind. They must be seen with the mind's eye and tested by practice and cultivation. If the reader treats any sentence without careful attention, all the sutras and all the treatises are futile. He is like one who gulps down his tea and cannot taste it. How can a reader enter the middle way when he tears through this book? The sutra says, "Enter the state of mindfulness by listening and thinking, practice and cultivation." How true!

Because the articles recount my personal

experiences, I cannot avoid being at their center. It may seem imprudent for me to dwell upon my life and times, but the readers should note that the purpose of these articles is not to praise the author, but to focus public attention upon large issues of critical importance. My sole wish is to serve the public.

Some important incidents and persons reappear in later articles, though seen from a different perspective. Rather than mere repetitions, they allow you to examine several aspects of a single phenomenon. If you are able to think twice about a critical issue, and enjoy viewing it from various positions, you will find something new every time.

I would like to thank the scholars and professional people who have recommended this series in their writings. I welcome all comments by the readers.

At the beginning of the new millenium, I am thankful for the blessings of the Triple Gem. I offer these books in celebration of the two thousand year history of the expansion of Buddhism in the East.

Hsing Yun
Founder's Quarter,
Fo Guang Shan, Taiwan
July 1999

Acknowledgments

One vital sentence can change your life. The *Hundred Sayings Series* rests on a hundred monumental sentences, each the foundation of a life-transforming article by the Venerable Master Hsing Yun. Glowing with insight, these are the harvest of a life rich in experience and a mind steeped in wisdom. Thanks to Venerable Man Ho for her painstaking translation, Leon Roth for inspired editing, Doris Koegel-Roth for invaluable support, and Venerable Miao Guang for her good advice. Special thanks are due to Venerable Yung Ming, director of the Culture Council, and Venerable Tzu Chuang, head of the Overseas Supervising Committee of Fo Guang Shan, without whose support this translation would not have been possible.

There Is Time to Rest Forever

In the fifty years since I began untiringly to propagate Buddhism, I have preached on six continents. Many friends, worried for my health, have asked, "Why don't you take a rest?" "There will be a time I will rest forever," I always answered.

From childhood, I always liked to read biographies of celebrated people. When I am absorbed in the lives of people ancient and modern, foreign and Chinese, I have seen that success comes to the diligent and failure to the extravagant and lazy. For decades, I have traveled everywhere. After examining and comparing the cultures and customs of many countries, I have come to realize that people who live in industrially advanced countries tend to be cheerful and confident, while people in poor countries are often indolent and unproductive. I have also found that resolute and steadfast people lead happy and productive lives. I did many kinds of menial work when I was young. But as long as my work benefits people, none of the hardships I have had to undergo spoils the pleasure I derive from thinking back on all my labors. For this reason, I often counsel my disciples that diligence leads to virtue and wealth while laziness leads to sin and poverty.

"Heavenly constellations wheel around continuously; virtuous people should strive hard without end." The four seasons take their turn continuously; the planets move continuously. As a part of nature, how can we escape from motion and work? There is a saying, "Stagnant water gathers worms; a rolling stone gathers no moss." We need to be active and energetic. Diligence is the only way to follow the way of heaven and to enjoy peace and stability. Therefore, I always advise those who ask me to take care of my health, "Keeping busy is the way to take care of myself," because there will be a time for us to rest forever.

Venerable Master Chih Yi of the Sui dynasty [589-618 C.E.], reading the chapter on the Medicine Bodhisattva in the *Lotus Sutra*, realized that "the real diligence is the mental practice of self-denial." He became enlightened then and there. I am sorry that I lack the good fortune and virtue needed to realize the wisdom of the Buddha. During a half-century of monastic life and decades of hardships, I have learned that practice and cultivation are incomparably superior to the superficial life of suffering and happiness, failure and success. Persevering practice contains the brilliance of

Buddha nature and the strength of compassion and vow. It is better to die busy than to live at leisure. Too much rest is like hibernation, a waste of time.

I feel sorry when I see talented young people exchange a life of compassion and vow for a life of ritual. After mastering the Buddhist teachings, they prefer to confine themselves to a small cell where they chant the name of the Buddha, or meditate in the mountains to avoid a busy life, or build temples merely to recruit disciples and solicit offerings.

Let's look at the Buddha. After becoming enlightened, he traveled throughout India to spread his teachings. Even at eighty, he continued to exhaust himself to spread the teachings to both banks of the Ganges. Many Bodhisattvas have been diligent in their practice and cultivation for many lifetimes. They endure suffering and hardships to save sentient beings, and even sacrifice body and mind, country and family, with no regret. The sages, in the cycle of birth and death, are able to cultivate merit and do good because they have made up their minds to persevere without regret. We, as ordinary monastics, are short on wisdom and merit. There are endless sentient beings waiting for us to save, and endless Dharma ways waiting for us to learn. So how can we just sit there and enjoy the easy life? The recluse or the common practitioner cannot avert endless troubles and attain supreme enlightenment.

"It is a rare thing to be reborn as a human being and to hear the Dharma. We are lucky to have been born as human beings and to hear the Buddhist teachings." If we cannot take hold of the present moment to practice and cultivate diligently, but instead while away our time, we let down the devotees who support the Dharma. If, due to lack of practice and cultivation, we fall into the realms of suffering when we pass away, we will stand ashamed before all the Buddhas and Bodhisattvas, for they have compassionately guided us.

A disciple of mine, having just returned after many years learning at other temples, said to me with surprise,

"Master, why don't you look old?"

I replied, "I don't have time to get old."

Confucius said, "Being diligent, I even forget to eat. I am happy to forget sorrow, and I don't even know that I'm getting old."

Old age does not mean living many years, but thinking you are old. Some people are young, but their minds are old. They are like living corpses. Some senior citizens with white hair are very healthy and energetic. In the Eastern Han dynasty [25-220 C.E.], Ma Yuan fought on the battlefield at an advanced age. Movingly, he vowed to "die in battle". At eighty, Prime Minister Meir of Israel was still negotiating for peace, declaring confidently, "I am never worried about old age. Old age is like a plane flying in the storm. You cannot stop either storm or plane. It is better to be optimistic, and let it fly."

Whether you are entangled in the five desires and six senses, or gallop in the wind and storm, time is like flowing water that never returns. To carry out endless tasks in our brief lifetime, we must prepare ourselves spiritually to race against time. Therefore, I handle affairs efficiently, solving some difficult cases in an instant. That is why people say that my office is the center of "immediately handling cases". No matter how busy I am, I try my best to fulfill people's expectations. That is why I am sometimes called "express mail".

In my early years, I spread Buddhist teachings by foot and bicycle. Later, I went by train and car. Nowadays, I fly between continents. I am still very busy, but I lead a simple life. To save time for work, I wash my face quickly and shave my head in five minutes. I have long trained myself to adapt to every circumstance. Whether in an airplane or train, or in a busy city, I enjoy reading to gain new knowledge, and I push myself to make progress. As a student in Buddhist college, I learned to use the time I spent walking and waiting in line. I want never to waste my time. A couple minutes walking or between lectures can be spent planning or making calligraphy or making affinity with people. I am keen to spend a day as if it were a year, a week as if a lifetime. There is not enough time. How do I have time to feel old?

Sometimes I get letters from devotees who wish me "freedom from illness and trouble". But I don't even have time to get old, let alone to be ill or troubled. The *Vimalakirti-nirdesa Sutra* says, "I am ill for sentient beings." The Ch'an Master Chao Chou said, "The Buddha is defilement; defilement is the Buddha." The practitioner of Bodhisattva realizes that everyone is endowed with the Buddha nature, and that there should be no discrimination between sentient beings. So he regards the illness and trouble of sentient beings as his own. Thus, he is perfectly willing to serve sentient beings like cattle or horse.

I entered monasticism at a young age, and studied Buddhist teachings day and night. I have emulated the sages by teaching continuously, bringing joy to others, and helping free them from intimidation. I never dare be lazy or complain. I feel the Dharma joy that others feel, which is like the joy of meditation. I benefit others with the benefits I have gained. Because I have felt for many years that when I work for others I work for myself, I am always immersed in work. Difficulties have never discouraged me. Though ill, I enjoy working.

When I broke my leg several years ago, many people showed their concern.

"Master, your feet are frail. Don't walk too much."

Even if I cannot walk, I can use my hands. Didn't the ancients say, "Hands are omnipotent"?

Time flies. During these years I have traveled around the earth several times. To raise funds for Hsi Lai and Fo Guang Universities, I have written over a thousand pieces of calligraphy for charity auctions.

Lately, my eyesight has been failing. My doctor warned me that unless I took care of my eyes I could become blind. Consequently, many admonitions rang in my ears.

"Master, your eyesight is getting worse. Don't work too hard."

Even if my eyes lose their function, I have a mouth. With a mouth, I can accumulate plenty of merits.

During these years, I have read over a thousand articles and given innumerable lectures.

Half a year ago (in 1995), my heart ailment was worsening and my breathing became labored. It made me realize that life lies just between our breaths, and that I cannot rest at random. I must push myself to work hard to propagate the Dharma.

After surgery, my disciples visited me and said,

"Master, your heart is frail. Don't fatigue yourself."

Though the physical heart is damaged, how can there be any impact on the true heart? As long as one is determined, one can succeed in anything.

They tried to persuade me, "Take a good rest so you can walk farther." It sounded reasonable at first. But "rest" doesn't necessarily help you "walk farther". Many people shut their eyes to sleep at night, but their minds linger on daytime affairs. So they toss and turn and cannot enjoy a good sleep. By day, their six senses go outward. A good rest is impossible. They may even incur defilement that disturbs their emotions at work. The real rest should "calm down" the six sensory organs and "terminate" all deluded thoughts. If we are able to do that, our true minds will appear. Then, it is possible to further exercise the sensory organs and sense objects to transform consciousness into wisdom, and to benefit sentient beings. Then, we can attain the state in which we rest when we work and are active when we rest. The Maha-stama-prapta Bodhisattva is adept at always controlling the six sensory organs and keeping a pure thought. Thus, the Bodhisattva can attain supreme mindfulness, and be omnipresent in the chanting of the name of the Buddha. Because Avalokitesvara Bodhisattva has attained the status of non-discrimination, she is able to answer thousands of prayers and be the ferry of salvation in the sea of suffering. I feel ashamed that my practice and cultivation are not equal to those of the Bodhisattvas. But because I always keep a tranquil mind, I can listen and reply, read a letter, and eat, all at the same time. I can approach everyone around me. When taping a television program in the studio I can recite a series of Dharma proverbs and stories without notes, finishing on time without seeing the clock. I have never had to do it over. That is why I often say that as long as we are tranquil at work, we can rest while working and work while resting. As long as we are detached, we can adapt to any circumstance. Even when we come under pressure, we can handle it with ease.

The aim of life is to improve the welfare of the universe. For that, it is not necessary to walk far. Venerable Seng Chao died young, but his *Treatise of Seng Chao*, written shortly after Buddhism reached China, is a treasure. Though Tsai Er lived just thirty years, he courageously exposed a conspiracy to destroy the young Republic, established in 1911, and prevented the restoration of the empire. That saved millions from despotism. Though the morning dew stays a fleeting moment, it nurtures the earth. The winter sun, though brief, melts frost and ice. While we live, we should endeavor to leave a brilliant light for posterity. There will be time for us to rest forever.

The ancient sages made vows and practiced diligently. Unwilling to waste even a second, they persisted to the end. Venerable Master Tao An passed away while lecturing; his disciple, Venerable Master Hui Yuan, passed away while chanting the name of the Buddha. Venerable Master Hsuan Tsang passed away while translating the sutra. Venerable Master Fo Yin passed away while receiving guests. I am already seventy years old, and I appreciate the laws of nature. Birth and death, honor and humiliation are like wind and cloud to me. But death can be as grand as a mountain or as slight as a feather. I hope I am lucky enough to make a grand death by passing away while busy at work.

Death looks to us like the end of life. But it is not really the end. When we die, and our bodies decay, consciousness remains to transmigrate with karmic energy. As ordinary human beings, we have undergone endless cycles of birth and death from time immemorial. We may be born as horses or cattle, or fall to hell or to the realm of hungry ghosts. When do we rest? But ordinary people ignorantly commit evil deeds, such as killing, stealing, sexual misconduct, and others. Owing to the bad karma, they cannot be peaceful in this life, but must suffer in the coming one. Venerable Kuei Shan is great because he vowed to serve as a buffalo in the coming life. When the Buddha was practicing in his previous lives, even as a bird or other animal he compassionately made great Mahayana vows to save endless beings. I am not so virtuous or able, but I have a compassionate heart. I vow to be reborn to this saha world as a monk, again and again, to spread the Buddhist teachings and save sentient beings.

Consider the wonderful sayings of Venerable Huang Po, a renowned Ch'an Master,

"When you show a thought of purity, you are the Dharmakaya[1] of your house.

"When your mind is devoid of discrimination, you are Sambhogakaya[2] of your house.

"When your mind is bright, you are Nirmanakaya[3] of your house."

Everyone is endowed with the Buddha nature. We don't have to seek it outside. Do not think that pleasure, or any manifestation of the Buddhas and Bodhisattvas, will save us in the coming life. We should strive to cultivate our Buddha nature, to vow to be the incarnation of all the Buddhas, and to abide by the spirit of the Bodhisattvas, who never rest. In the arena of the world we can

---

[1] The Dharmakaya is, like space, unclassifiable, and nothing can be said about it.

[2] The Sambhogakaya is awe-inspiring, gigantic, and glorious. It is a celestial or divine form. It is capable of moving through the universe at will, for it does not depend on the laws of physics as human experience them.

[3] The Nirmanakaya is the human form. It looks, feels, smells, sleeps, eats, walks, laughs, and cries just like a human.

endlessly benefit others and ourselves. Soon enough we shall rest forever. Why don't we seize this moment to dedicate ourselves to strenuous effort?

Don't Compare and Haggle with Others

T en years ago, twin brothers Chih-chi Lee and Chih-hsi Lee asked me, through Ms. Chih-min Chou, for a specimen of my calligraphy. On a piece of rice paper, I wrote, "Don't compare and haggle with each other." Afterwards, they made peace with each other and earned a good deal of recognition in the entertainment industry. One disciple asked me, "How did you come up with the slogan?" Instead of answering his question, I asked him, "What is the source of defilement in our lives?" After thinking about it awhile, he replied, "Comparing and haggling with others."

The defilement and ignorance do indeed come from "comparing and haggling". A baby uses his sense of touch to "compare" those who love him most. Through crying, he displays his "comparison". When he goes to school, he "compares" his test scores with those of his classmates and "haggles" whether teachers are impartial. When he grows up and goes to work, he "compares" his wages to those of other employees and questions whether the boss is fair. After his parents pass away, he even "compares" himself with his siblings as to who will get a larger inheritance, and "haggles" whether his parents' will is impartial. Through "comparing and haggling", discrimination and disputes arise. This often leads to tragedy, as when siblings become enemies who may even kill each other.

Earlier in this century, Ching-wei Wang was not so fortunate as to be chairman of the nationalist government, as Kai-shek Chiang was. Because of his "comparing and haggling" mentality, he cooperated with Japanese to arrange a "government of peace". He afterwards regretted having to be called a traitor. When I read history, I feel sorry for those who committed wrong, and I am vigilant for myself. I am over seventy years of age. Reflecting on my life, I feel that I was lucky not to be born with the character of "comparing and haggling" with others.

When I was a child, my parents were often not at home. Having an older and a younger brother and an older sister, I took the initiative in cooking, cleaning, and buying the daily necessities. Because I didn't "haggle" about the amount and the complexity of my work, I could do plenty at the age of eight or nine. Learning to do my job well helped me later on with getting along and handling affairs.

I entered monasticism at twelve and studied at the Buddhist college. Life was hard then. I never had a chance to wear new clothes, just those of the departed. I never had enough food, and ate rice once every two weeks. The broth was clean as water, without oil or vegetable. In the big monastery, it was not unusual to be mistreated. The conservative monastic education included frequent scolding. But my ten years passed quickly. While many monastics quit halfway, I regarded the training "as it should be". I didn't indulge in gossip or "haggle" about the treatment. Consequently, I could learn and practice with a tranquil mind and benefit from the Dharma joy.

According to the ancient sage, "It is not difficult to walk the ultimate t'ao (way); the only way is to avoid being hard to please." When I first read this at a young age, I couldn't understand it. Now I realize its truth. Looking at youth today, I see that it is hard for them to enter the gateway of Buddhism because they wish everything to be pleasant and reasonable. A harsh word or a hard look upsets them. Without determination to practice and cultivate, how can they succeed? In my view, the proper attitude is to be considerate of others and make concessions to benefit everyone. It is practical to work for everyone's interest. On the principle of "not to compare and haggle with others", we can follow the middle way, getting along and handling affairs well.

Master Chih K'ai intended to assign me as a receptionist in Ch'i-hsia Temple after my graduation from Chiao-shan Buddhist College. Ch'i-hsia is where I was tonsured, and the receptionist is one of the four pillars of the Temple. I was obliged to repay the favors of the Temple, but I was glad to accept the task as a way to test myself. Unexpectedly, I was appointed deacon in meditation hall. Though I was not good at meditation, I didn't "compare" my position with others or "haggle" whether my job was too hard. By assuming it cheerfully and meditating intensely, I gained precious experience while learning how to meditate. Now, I often advise my disciples that they should gain experience through being assigned to a variety of departments in the spirit of "not comparing and haggling". That would help assure their future success.

In 1949, political conditions in China were chaotic when I left for Taiwan with the Sangha Relief Group. After several frustrating experiences, I settled in Chungli. I worked hard to repay the temple, but my hard work aroused jealousy. Whenever there was a difficult task, some fellow monastics would say, "Let Hsing Yun do it because he is strong." I remember always being overworked to the point of dizziness and vomiting, but I persisted. Afterwards, the abbot Venerable Miao Kuo recognized my merit. He took me to many places to propagate Buddhist teachings, and even asked me to manage a temple. I turned down his request because I didn't want a high position. Now, when I reflect on the source of Hsing Yun's strength, I think it is just that I am never bothered by gossip and never calculate gain or loss. That is why I can persist in my work.

In 1951, I was invited to be dean of studies of the Taiwan Buddhist training program in Ch'ing-ts'ao Lake, Hsinchu. One day a monk yelled in panic, "My Buddha! There are over twenty abbots from mainland China." I was glad to hear that and replied to him, "Great! They build temples everywhere. We will have room and board wherever we go." How wonderful it is to embrace the ideal of sharing honors and co-existence by "not comparing" our achievements with others and "not haggling" about owning something? Subsequently, when I was solicited for funds to build a retirement home in Singapore, I complied even though Fo Guang Shan's financial condition left it stranded in the early construction stage.

In the same year, I was invited by Venerable Tung Ch'u to edit *Life Monthly*. For the next six years, I voluntarily wrote articles, handled anything related to editing, and even paid for postage and transportation. I was never concerned whether my name appeared in the magazine, or that my task was more difficult than that of others. I felt it was important to shoulder the duty to spread Buddhist teachings everywhere, through cultural undertakings, at a time when Buddhism was on the decline. Later on, Venerable Tung Ch'u put my name in the magazine as "printer". Though it was not true, I didn't mind. Subsequently, many newspapers, magazines, and radio stations invited me to write Buddhist material. I worked for them without charge. For fifty years, I have watched Buddhism flourish, and seen many deluded people saved. I realize that having something is not the same as owning something, and that have-not is not necessarily having nothing. Only when we "do not compare and haggle" with others can we devote our limited span of life to infinite time and space, and leave behind a contribution to the everlasting.

It is easier "not to compare" rich or poor, and

"not to haggle" having or not. The most difficult thing is to be tranquil in the face of loss and humiliation. In the early years of this century, Venerable Jen Shan followed Venerable Master T'ai Hsu in reforming Buddhism. He was celebrated in Chin-shan Temple for an extraordinary incident. When he went to Malaysia to spread Buddhist teachings, a monk who didn't know who he was said to him, "Do you know someone called Jen Shan, a seed of hell, in Chin-shan Temple? He has committed innumerable sins. He can only be found in the nineteenth story of hell[1] after he dies." On hearing this, Venerable Jen Shan offered the monk two silver dollars and said, "You are right." After that, he left quietly. For him, reformation of Buddhism was essential, but it was not necessary to take others' words and actions too seriously.

At that time, Venerable Ta Hsing was one of the eminent students of Venerable Master T'ai Hsu. He was controversial because he criticized the conservative monastic system in the *Modern Sangha* magazine. One day, he went to Ling-yen-shan Temple in Suchou for an audience with Venerable Master Yin Kuang, the thirteenth patriarch of Chinese Pureland school. Master Yin

---

[1] It's said that there are eighteen stories in hell.

Kuang reproached him. "You have committed negative verbal karma." Nevertheless, to preserve the teaching of Master Yin Kuang, Venerable Ta Hsing compiled and published a book of articles from the magazine, and titled it *Collections of Negative Verbal Karma*. This shows that he didn't calculate gain or loss, but was brave enough to speak for the future of Buddhism.

Venerable Master T'ai Hsu exposed, without complaint or resentment, the deep-rooted corrupt practices of Buddhism in his article *My Failure in the Reformation of Buddhism.* When, in my youth, I learned about the devoted works of the sages, I deeply admired their righteousness. After arriving in Taiwan and working on reformation, I came to realize the difficulty of their tasks.

Several decades ago, when the Taiwanese were quite conservative and Christianity was very popular, a curfew was still in effect. Just a bit of candid speech or a little reform of Buddhism was enough to shock people. Monastics were criticized for wearing a watch, using a fountain pen, or riding in a car. I was considered weird, and was threatened because I taught students basketball and organized a Buddhist youth choir. I was followed by police wherever I went to spread

Buddhist teachings, and was interrogated because I welcomed as teachers scholars who advocated free speech. Then I suffered a series of slanders that made me indignant. Thinking of the future of Buddhism, however, I pushed ahead and overcame many difficulties. Reflecting on the past, I realize that the way to succeed is to look at the whole picture and "not to compare and haggle" about petty matters. Success comes when there are good causes and conditions.

It cost me a great deal of time to establish new concepts. To promote new ideas required hard work and toleration of mistakes. In 1958, when my book *The Biography of Sakyamuni Buddha* was made into a movie in Taiwan, I accepted the producers' invitation to serve as technical advisor. Despite my inexperience, I was ready to help. But, I didn't read the script in detail. After it was released, the movie provoked violent reactions because it depicted certain improper acts. Many Buddhist followers came to our new Buddhist Culture Service Center to scold me, and threatened to demolish our office. When the movie was shown in Malaysia, many monks demonstrated silently in front of the cinema. They too laid the blame on me. Although the producers knew I was wronged, I never complained to them. In my view, it was impossible from the start to shoot a perfect movie. Someone had to take responsibility, and it would have impeded the progress of Buddhism if we were afraid of reproach. Subsequently, Ms. Chuan Yu produced a soap opera titled *Biography of the Buddha*, based on my *Biography of Sakyamuni Buddha*. Again I suffered undeserved blame. But it was reasonable to think that the movie's mistakes would be corrected. So I patiently decided "not to haggle" about it. Lately, though, Buddhist movies have been improving.

Three years ago, Mr. Feng Kou produced a series of soap operas titled *A Love Affair After Transmigration,* based on my book *National Master Yu Lin*. It was a sensation both on local CTV and abroad. The actors, crew, and many fans converted to Buddhism. Twenty years ago, when *National Master Yu Lin* was broadcast on air force radio as a literary novel, nobody recognized its worth. Nowadays, people have come to realize the importance of movies and television in propagating Buddhism. Isn't it wonderful not to surrender to a momentary failure?

One afternoon in 1994, Ms. Yu Chou visited me with a group of cameramen, to ask that I promote her new soap opera *Emperor T'ai Chung of the*

T'ang Dynasty. Though I was not happy about it, and expected to be criticized for doing it, I granted her unexpected request. Subsequently, many upset viewers called me or wrote to accuse me. But this modern medium offers Buddhism a way to convert masses of people. If we just "compare and haggle" about trifles, we waste our time and miss a chance. Nothing can go our way all the time. It is better to shoulder our responsibility and get on with it.

Forty years ago, when I just started to spread Buddhist teachings in Ilan, I worked very hard to educate the obstinate. Mr. Sung-nien Lin came of age when Taiwan was ruled by Japan, and he had therefore acquired many of the bad habits of the militarists. Whenever he entered my room, he first kicked the door open and treated me rudely. Mr. Hsiu-yun Hsiung was persuaded by his uncle to come to one of my lectures. As I began to speak, this arrogant intellectual folded his arms skeptically across his chest. I was just a newcomer, and knew I had challenges ahead. I didn't want to calculate gain or loss. I only wanted to do my best to help the multitude learn and practice Buddhist teachings. So I got along and handled affairs with the mind of equanimity. In the end, everyone became faithful devotees who supported Buddhism with all their hearts. In a sense, I have never left Ilan.

It is said that, "Those in the same trade despise each other." But many of my fellow monastics were my good friends. We helped and encouraged each other. Venerable Chu Yun was my classmate at Ch'i-hsia Buddhist College. Never "comparing and haggling" with each other, we became intimate friends. In January 1933, an old devotee in the Ilan chanting group told me that Venerable Chu Yun was going to Fengshan, Kaohsiung in February, but that he preferred to stay in Ilan. He hoped that I could go to Fengshan in his place. I gladly agreed to go, because we were good friends. But unexpectedly, the devotees of Fengshan welcomed Venerable Chu Yun with such warmth, that he decided to settle there.

In 1964, I established Shou-shan Buddhist College in Shou-shan Temple and invited Venerable Chu Yun to teach there. When there was fruit offered by devotees, a newspaper on the table, or fine food in the kitchen, his attendant would collect it for him. My disciples complained several times, but I always said, "Venerable Chu Yun and I have been good friends for decades. Now he is willing to live with me, and I have nothing good to offer. So don't make a fuss about trifles."

Many fellow monastics called him "Venerable VIP, Middle, and Front". When we ate, he chose the VIP seat. When we took photos, he sat in the middle of the front row. When we walked, he automatically walked in front. But several times when we boarded transportation, he would fall back and let me pay. When my disciples complained about it, I told them, "Money is to be used. Don't worry about me."

Venerable Chu Yun was very good to me. When some fellow monastics backbit me in order to sow discord, he just laughed it off or said kind things about me. We had known each other well, and cherished our friendship until he passed away.

In 1955, I began building Kaohsiung Buddhist Temple. Abundant disputes arose from the start. I have never wanted to "compare and haggle" with others in handling affairs. My focus was on carrying out the mission. After completing the temple, I handed it over to my teacher, Venerable Yueh Chi, to serve as abbot.

When I founded Fo Guang Shan, I didn't know that it would be the foundation for over one hundred branch temples and organizations worldwide. On reflection, I realize that I play a role in Buddhism not because of my wisdom or ability, but because my disciples work as a team.

When I lecture around the world, many overseas Chinese ask how I attained my success. I always speak from experience: "Don't criticize self-interest. Serve the community and do your part, with others, to create a beautiful future."

Trees flourish and shelter birds because they can tolerate rain and wind. The ocean is broad and deep enough for sea animals because it does not shun streams. Human beings must be tolerant based on the spirit of "not comparing and haggling" with others. In Ch'an school Buddhism there is a saying, "Don't think of right or wrong." This tells us not to discriminate. According to the *Heart Sutra,* "no sight, sound, smell, taste, touch or conception ..." It tells us not to be attached to our surroundings. As long as we don't discriminate, we can follow causes and conditions and be as carefree as empty space.

*Keeping Busy Is
the Best Nourishment*

At a time when some of my disciples were ill and needed to rest at Jui Liao, Venerable Yung Chun, my driver and former director of the personnel department, said to me, "They look healthy and have nothing to do. Why are they ill? We are busy with several jobs, so why are we well?" I answered without thinking, "Keeping busy is the best nourishment." Surprisingly, this sentence passed among my disciples as Dharma words. But it is a fact that my body and mind are healthy because I have been very busy.

Since childhood, I have kept busy. As a boy I rose every day at cockcrow, transplanting rice seedlings, weeding, herding cows, and feeding chickens. I also kept busy playing with my friends -- catching mudfish, looking for grasshoppers, playing cards, and telling stories. I ate and slept in a hurry. Even ill, I was very busy. Keeping busy made me strong and persevering.

When I became a novice monk at twelve my lifestyle changed, but I was still very busy. There were morning and evening chanting, study, and temple chores such as carrying wood and fetching water, protecting the woods, searching the woods for thieves, and guarding the monastery gate. I was also busy making an enlightenment vow, enhancing my aspiration, chanting the name of the Buddha, making mental drafts, and more. I was busy doing everything I could do, no matter where I was, from morning till night. Keeping busy made my body and mind stronger and enabled me to make good affinity with others.

Because I regularly volunteered to work in a vegetable garden, the supervisor would give me some cabbages, sweet potatoes, and ginger. I used them to cook soup with noodles, which I gladly shared with my classmates. In the cold of winter I was especially content to crouch in a corner of the kitchen with a few good friends, busily eating noodles while hiding from the disciplinarian teacher. It kept me excited and warm, and it provided cherished memories.

I volunteered every month to wrap and mail *Chungliu* magazine, which was published by our monastery. Usually, after working an entire day, I would be applauded by my teachers and even given a copy. Reading for free was precious to me, poor as I was, and I was eager to read.

As a student at the Buddhist college, I was keen to cook for my fellow monastics and to work at our fabrics factory. Though I never ate more than the rest, nor was given any fabric, keeping busy made me realize how much hard work is needed to produce our worldly goods, and it gave me insight into the essence of dependent origination. That has benefited me all my life.

Keeping busy can be fun. It helped me enjoy peace and stability, both of body and mind. A busy life was a joy because it gave me understanding and experience, and showed me the defects of an idle life.

I once hid a nest of newborn rats in a drawer, in order to care for them in secret. I chewed their rice every day before feeding it to them, and I watched their naked skin become covered with black shiny hair. At first they were quiet, with eyes tightly shut, but later they became quite lively as they jumped about. They made me feel the preciousness of life. As the wisest of creatures, how can we not keep as busy as they?

Once, a classmate gave me some silkworms. After class and temple chores I went to the mountain every day for mulberry leaves. I had to feed the silkworms while avoiding discovery by my teachers. I watched them build cocoons and later emerge as butterflies. These experiences taught me how to keep busy in a leisurely way, and encouraged my future vocation, which would be spreading Buddhist teachings.

As librarian of the Buddhist college I worked hard to put the collection in order. When I had spare time, I read distinguished Chinese and foreign books, such as *Shui-hu Chuan,*[1] *The Count of Monte Cristo,* and *Romance of the Three Kingdoms.* At bedtime I hid in my comforter, reading by the light of burning incense until dawn. In my lifelong study, I have read many books and cultivated a great interest in literature.

My teachers kept me busy mimeographing handouts for my classmates. My classmates kept me busy sorting and binding them. Keeping busy earned me recognition from teachers and elders and won friends. Keeping busy made me realize the importance of teamwork and the meaning of concerted efforts. In a conservative mountain monastery I had no chance to read the *Guidelines for Youth*, but I could recognize that helping others is the source of happiness. Avalokitesvara Bodhisattva has been busy answering the calls of suffering beings twenty-four hours a day, and

---

[1] A classic novel about Thirteenth Century China, whose one hundred and eight characters are compelled to flee the social chaos of the decaying Sung dynasty. Its author is thought to be Nai-an Shih. There are many English translations.

Ksitigarbha Bodhisattva has been busy saving the inmates in hell. For that they have been greatly praised and revered by Buddhists. Clearly, keeping busy generates good deeds, benefits others, is a gesture of friendship, and is meritorious. Keeping busy is the essence of Buddhism.

The Lu-kou Bridge Incident of 1937 triggered the Sino-Japanese War, which ended in 1945. That was succeeded by the conflict between nationalists and communists. For more than ten years I and other suffering Chinese were busy wandering and seeking shelter, escaping bullets and air attacks, and helping the injured, the departed, the orphans, and the aged. Quitting the mountain monastery enabled me to lead a monastic life, and at the same time to gain an education, embrace the urban multitude, and afterwards leave the war behind to spread Buddhist teachings in Taiwan.

When I began lecturing, I had to devote busy nights to preparation. Writing an article demanded busy nights racking my brain. Though I was never paid for my lectures or articles, I felt a great sense of achievement when I saw my audiences grow larger, when they nodded or applauded in appreciation, and when my articles were printed in the magazines *Bodhi Tree*, *Life Monthly*, *Awakening the Masses*, and *Free Youth*. This kind of happiness is far beyond a life of luxury. When I was busy, I felt the Dharma joy of service and dedication that seeks nothing in return. That is why I can adapt myself to have or have-not, happiness or suffering, superiority or inferiority, advance or retreat.

When I had to publish a book without delay, I lived a month in a hut in a remote mountain area, sleeping on the ground, the earth my table, dedicated to writing down the ideal of humanistic Buddhism. By the time I finished for the day, the sky had turned white like the belly of the fish, for it was well past midnight. I suffered hunger many times when walking from Tali Street to Wanhua railroad station, then riding the train to Old Peitou and the bus to New Peitou, and then walking to the mountaintop in the dark, merely to hand a new copy of a magazine to an elder. Only then could I relax. Though I was extremely busy, I never felt that something was lost, but rather that my faith and aspiration had been enhanced.

In 1951, I was dean of studies of the Taiwan Buddhist training program. I had to rise early and go to bed late. I was busy leading students in morning and evening chanting sessions, doing temple chores, preparing teaching materials, and grading students' papers and exercises. In addition, I was busy reading more than eighty students' diaries and keeping their lives on the right track. I lost five kilograms (eleven pounds) that month. Keeping busy gradually expanded my mind and vision. Keeping busy develops our potential and reveals our buried treasure. I use being busy to increase my diligence and motivation.

Four or five decades ago life was hard. The ancients said, "Study leads to golden mansions and beauty." It has also been said, "Teaching leads to enjoying noodles with mushrooms and good offerings." In my view, the fun of teaching did not lie in beautiful clothes and delicious food, but in inculcating right concepts to students. So, whenever I got money for my articles or chanting services, I bought Buddhist books to share with devotees. Performing vital tasks is far better than enjoying golden houses, beauty, noodles with mushrooms, or good offerings. I often spent a whole day on the train from Ilan to Kaohsiung, just to give a lecture, and then rode the overnight train back to Ilan. Riding back and forth took a lot of my time, but it was a joy because it strengthened me. Besides my regular lectures, I was busy lecturing to factory workers and instructing fishermen, presiding over refuge ceremonies for prisoners, and talking to officers and soldiers in military camps. Some people said their days were long and tedious, but my twenty-four hour days passed too quickly, and I could have wished that my days contained forty-eight hours.

After taxi service was inaugurated, I sometimes had to use it. As the mileage rose my heart would sink. It was no pleasure being busy while trying to save money. But when I saw the glad faces of my audiences, or did my job well, I was happy beyond measure.

Since the 1960s, many universities have organized Buddhist clubs, and Buddhist radio programs have been broadcast. I was getting busier and busier. I not only served temples but also lectured to Buddhists. I taught students and wrote for radio. I was spinning like a top for the whole day. But I was happy with my busy life.

I used to go to various temples for inauguration ceremonies or installation of abbots. Nor did I hesitate to join in funerals, weddings, and other services. Soon I found myself compelled to waste time socializing. Though I chose to keep busy hobnobbing rather than cause disappointment, I could not always satisfy people's expectations.

Before fame came to me, I relished the pleasure of being busy. But after I became famous, keeping busy sometimes became a burden. It is clear that fame is an encumbrance. What tired me out was not the effort but my reluctance to disappoint people. Nevertheless, though it was impossible to manage every situation satisfactorily, I still loved to keep myself busy.

After my fiftieth year, as well as promoting Buddhism I took up yet another project. I have written down my history of "keeping busy". During the course of my life, I have established temples for monastics to cultivate and practice in; founded Buddhist colleges, senior citizens' homes, and nurseries; and written and edited books and magazines. I have employed every means to teach stubborn children, and exhausted myself to persuade an obstinate old man. Time flies when I am busy thinking or working. The sutra says, "Work on Buddhist undertakings and never take a rest." When I was busy educating sentient beings, I learned to be modest and patient, and cultivated my compassion and tolerance. It has produced a great harvest in my life.

In the early construction stage of Fo Guang Shan, I was busy cultivating the fields with my disciples. On weekdays, I was busy sweeping fallen leaves. On weekends, I was busy in the kitchen cooking vegetarian meals for visitors. When there was a flood, I was busy protecting the temple with my body. After the flood, I was busy with soil conservation. When the typhoon came, I was busy inspecting everything. After the typhoon, I was busy repairing the fallen hut. According to the sutra, "In a grain of sand we can see a world; in a leaf, a Tathagata." In my busy life, I realized the essence of this teaching through my devotion to every bit of soil and leaf of Fo Guang Shan.

I have spent the past decade spreading the teachings worldwide. I have made six pilgrimages to India and eight visits to Europe to teach the Dharma. I have made seven trips to Australia and New Zealand, and three to Brazil, Argentina, and other countries of South America, to inspect our temples. To spread Mahayana teachings to the West, I have gone to the United States and Canada more than thirty times. I have traveled to Hong Kong for over fifteen consecutive years, to attend the three-day lecture series. On April 21st, 1996, I spoke to eighty thousand people at the Shah Alam Stadium in Malaysia. I even went to Ladakh, India, ascending to an elevation of 4,000 meters to spread the teachings. I have been to United Nations headquarters, the office of the president of India, the Royal Palace in Thailand, and the White House in Washington, to meet with world leaders. I have seen the marvelous Three Gorges of the Yangtze River and the Seven Wonders of the World. In my busy schedule, I took time to visit Red Square in Moscow, and I went to Sweden to discover the peace and happiness of its social democracy. At NASA, in Texas, I grasped the achievements of space technology, and at Universal Studios, in California, I gained a deeper understanding of the function of movies. As a global person, I have been busy spreading happiness everywhere and immersing myself in everything. Every day of my life is busy and happy.

A rolling stone gathers no moss; flowing water gathers no worms. Keeping busy enables one to show the strength of life. Keeping busy makes our bodies and minds lively. According to the sutra, "A lazy practitioner is like one who drills for fire, but gives up before the fire comes. There is no way to make the fire." The sutra also says, "If one drills persistently for water, the fountain will flow." Keeping busy can mobilize us for success. If we are good at keeping ourselves busy, it will be the best nourishment for a healthy and happy life.

Even the Buddha
  Was Slandered

Throughout my life, I have suffered uncounted slanders. My strenuous efforts to improve the welfare of humanity have often been misunderstood. Though I tried to put up with derision when I was young, those false accusations always filled me with sorrow. Even now, this distortion of my good intentions sometimes distresses me.

In 1963, I was a member of a Chinese Buddhist group making its first visit to Southeast Asia. At our final destination, a fellow monk suggested that because we had to carry home a lot of gifts, it would be best to return by ship. I replied, "We had best fly, since the government wired that they would pick us up at the airport." Unexpectedly, after we returned to Taiwan that monk wrote in a Buddhist magazine that Hsing Yun wanted to return by ship because he had bought lots of goods for sale, etc. But a monk who knew the facts comforted me: "Don't be upset. Even the Buddha was slandered. People's minds are as different as their looks. Whenever someone agrees with something, he feels that is true, kind, and beautiful. But if he does not agree, he will say that is ugly and demonic. Sometimes, slander can be a kind of nourishment." I was happy to hear this. Thereafter, whenever I was slandered, I would think of the compassionate and tolerant spirit of the Buddha. That encouraged me to move forward. Nowadays, I often share my experiences with my disciples. "Even the Buddha was slandered." I hope they will be forbearing as they labor to spread the Dharma for the benefit of sentient beings.

Ever since I went to Ilan in 1954, I have devoted my time and best efforts to Lei-yin Temple. The devotees there have not always supported me. Whenever someone suggested that I take over administration of Lei-yin Temple, some devotees would oppose it on the ground that I am from the mainland. It never bothered me, because I thought a monk should be determined to spread Buddhist teachings everywhere. Therefore, besides handling temple affairs, I studied hard in my spare time. I vowed to be a global person embracing all sentient beings. Slander reminded me to examine myself and be firm in my goal.

Ten years ago, I went to Los Angeles for the first time to examine the possibility of spreading Buddhism there. I carried a magnificent Buddha statue that I donated to Venerable Hsuan Hua, who was spreading the teachings in California. When I returned to Los Angeles to build Hsi Lai Temple, I discovered that he had written to the county that all monks from Taiwan were fakes. After ten hard years, we completed construction of the temple and realized our wish to spread the teachings to Americans. The Buddha statue remained in Chin-lun Temple, where it seemed to attest the truth of history.

When Hsi Lai Temple was near completion, an abbot from New York said to me, "You don't speak English. You can do nothing in the West. Let me take charge of the Temple." I didn't reply, but I believed that spreading the teachings to the West depends on the vow and compassion, not knowledge of English. Several years later, with the acceptance of Hsi Lai Temple, we established others in the eastern and central United States, and the Canadian cities of Toronto, Vancouver, Montreal, Edmonton, and Ottawa. We also have temples in Brazil, Paraguay, and Argentina. In Europe, temples have been built in France, the United Kingdom, Germany, Holland, and Switzerland. These carry out the mission of benefiting sentient beings. In my view, in this chaotic world of gossip and error, we should leap yet higher and farther, like a balloon in flight, after slanderous attacks.

When I was in Los Angeles in 1990, I was invited for a live interview on the radio program *Voice of Chinese.* I was interviewed by the host, Mr. Pa Shan, and answered callers' questions. A minister, heedless of the audience's protest, talked on and on against Buddhism and tried to convert Pa Shan to Christianity. Later, he said to me, "Master, it is the strength granted by God that enables you to build the magnificent Hsi Lai Temple." I retorted at once, "It is fine for you to believe in Christianity. I agree with you that Jesus Christ is great. But it is the donation and support of thousands of overseas devotees that makes the construction of Hsi Lai Temple possible. This honor cannot be credited to God, but to the Buddha." Finally, I politely invited him to visit Hsi Lai Temple. As I was leaving, the atheist Pa Shan said to me, "Master, if I'm going to believe in a religion, I'll believe in Buddhism."

In the *Sutra of Forty-two Sections,* the Buddha said, "To smear others is like spitting towards the sky. The spit falls back on your face and does not touch the sky. If you want to smear a victim by throwing dust against the wind, the dust besmears the thrower, not the target." It's true! "A virtuous person is open and frank, while a mean person is always gloomy." As long as we are upright and brilliant like the sun, the slander will soon vanish like the frost.

In April 1992, I led nine disciples on an around-the-world Dharma preaching trip. In Malaysia, a local monk criticized me in a newspaper article that generated much disharmony. He claimed that Taiwanese Buddhism was full of regionalism, that the concept of "one teacher and one way" was designed to enchain devotees, and that our aim in Malaysia was to establish a colonial Buddhism. We laughed when we read it. Buddhism in China and India comprises many schools and groups. That does not guarantee schism. The profundity of Buddhist teachings requires that they be sorted out in order to diffuse to the world the core meaning of each school. Multi-faceted development propels the progress of Buddhism. It does not impede it.

Consider the four celebrated mountains of China, which symbolize the great Bodhisattvas: Avalokitesvara, Manjusri, Ksitigarbha, and Samantabhadra. Each Bodhisattva is famed for his particular attribute — compassion, wisdom, vow, or practice. Can we say that they are regional? Buddhism has advocated "one teacher and one way" since antiquity. It aims to lead us on the path of the Buddha, and to avoid false teachers. "One teacher and one way" promotes harmony. It is not peculiar to Buddhism. Christianity and Islam also support it. I wonder why the monk criticized us in such an absurd way. No wonder we all laughed!

As for colonial Buddhism, I have never heard of it. Buddhism spread from India to China, then to the rest of Asia. Incorporating local culture and customs, Buddhism became a religion tinged with local features. Nobody then called it colonial Buddhism. Besides Buddhism, other religions expanded abroad without being scorned as colonial religions. Therefore, it is obvious that the accusation was biased against Buddhism.

When my disciple Hui Hai was appointed to run our branch temples in his native Malaysia, he was widely criticized for many of his actions. With a firm determination to spread Buddhist teachings to benefit sentient beings, he overcame these challenges to win acclaim. When I lectured eighty thousand people at Shah Alam Stadium in Kuala Lumpur in 1996, it was sensational. This shows that slander cannot defeat someone who embraces great aspiration and ideal.

Thirty years ago, when I was building the Buddha Hall at Fo Guang Shan, someone said contemptuously, "Now is the *mo-fa*[1] and Buddhism is declining. Of what use is a magnificent Buddha Hall?" I think that in our chaotic society we must build majestic temples that instruct without words. When completed, its grandeur drew many visitors. It was so remarkable that the builder of the Grand Hotel asked us to share our blueprints. Later on, I was criticized because I carpeted the guestrooms, lecture halls, and conference rooms, and installed air-conditioners. Our temple in central Taiwan was criticized for extravagance because it possesses golden-edged tables made of plywood.

All purelands of the Buddhist sutras are paved with gold, and furnished with buildings and pavilions of seven treasures, and birds that teach. Modern institutions must cater to people's needs with beautiful and comfortable surroundings. Now, many people come to enjoy our lectures, and government officials even hold conferences in our temples. That is why we should pay attention to slander and use it as a touchstone of our faith and practice.

---

[1] The last of the three formal periods of the Buddhist teachings, in which its deterioration will lead to its eventual extinction. The first period was *cheng-fa* (period of correct doctrine) and the second was *hsiang-fa* (semblance period).

Several years ago, a reporter asked me, "Why does Fo Guang Shan display Buddha statues made of concrete, since concrete reflects a coarseness of culture?" I know that there has been great progress in the evolution of materials. The Copper Age followed the Stone Age, etc. This is the age of steel bars and cement. It would be strange if we built with other materials than steel bars and cement. I have advocated, "Decorate with wisdom, not with money." If I make Buddha statues of gold, silver, copper, or iron, I cannot afford new buildings. But devotees and pilgrims have always paid their respects to the Buddhas, not the concrete. People come a long way to Fo Guang Shan to see the Buddhas, not the material they are made from. Slander reveals the weakness of human nature, and teaches a lesson we can all understand.

Since the Buddha's time, the gravest slander to Buddhism is that monastics are not productive. In truth, monastics spread Buddhist teachings to benefit sentient beings, purifying minds. That is the most beneficial and productive kind of work. For the past three decades, my disciples have undertaken charity, administration, lecturing, and editing. I dare not say that we have contributed greatly. But at least we have worked harder than others in society, and our transcendent attitudes help solve society's problems.

Some charge that Fo Guang Shan organizes too many worldly activities and falls short in practice and cultivation. In fact, twenty-six hundred years ago the Buddha followed custom when he led his disciples in collecting alms from devotees, repaying them with public lectures.

Since Buddhism entered China, monastics have successively performed agricultural and industrial work, supplied vegetarian food, and offered chanting services, travel assistance, and care for the seriously ill. Besides charity and educational and cultural enterprises, monastics have run pawnshops, warehouses, rice-husking mills, and others. These have facilitated economic growth and enhanced humanistic cultivation. In our day, we have founded all sorts of Buddhist enterprises and organized all kinds of activities that systematically benefit sentient beings. All monastics of Fo Guang Shan rise at 4:30 a.m.[2] In addition to morning and evening chanting, and caring for their surroundings, they are busy benefiting the public

---

[2] Since the end of year 2000, the time to rise has been changed to 5:30 a.m. because monastics usually are busy and work late.

from morning till evening. What can be called a busy life of practice and cultivation, if not this?

When I started advocating humanistic Buddhism, many sneered behind my back, or accused me to my face of merely craving attention. Years later, many people now follow our teachings. Scholars in China, Russia, and elsewhere have done research on humanistic Buddhism. We know that people sometimes slander us out of ignorance. We should advance our ideals with words, and prove their value by actions.

Forty years ago, I was criticized for regularly bringing a group of young people to the countryside for Dharma preaching. Gradually, we gained approval through our deportment and good work. Now many parents would prefer to have me teach their children about Buddhism.

When bhiksunis (nuns) were still disdained, I tried to raise their status, despite ridicule by monks who called me "commander of the female working group". Some of them called bhiksunis parasites of Buddhism. Nevertheless, they won grudging respect for their hard work. Now, we have many learned, eloquent bhiksuni professionals who write and teach in universities and Buddhist colleges. The *Fo Guang Buddhist Dictionary* was compiled by bhiksunis. Their achievements have won praise and defied slander.

In 1973, during the scandal at the department of philosophy of National Taiwan University, many professors were fired, including Ku-ying Chen, Jih-chang Lee, and others who had taught in our Buddhist college. It was the time of the curfew. I suggested to those scholars that they devote themselves to academic research, where they could think freely but did not have to act. Subsequently, rumors spread that "Fo Guang Shan is a communist camp", "Fo Guang Shan hides over two thousand rifles", "Fo Guang Shan is financed by communists". Investigators came often to interrogate us. Twenty-two years later, an inquiry by a panel of six professors from National Taiwan University took two years to uncover the truth and vindicate the innocent. Fo Guang Shan's loyalty has long passed the test of time, and is no longer in doubt. Slander cannot harm our image for long, but in the end it always reveals our greatness.

Some decades ago, people were afraid to be accused of social and intellectual transgressions. Now, the curfew is gone, but certain charges are still made. You may be called a "business monk" or a "political monk". Even the media use this line to shock the public. Several years ago, a magazine writer attempted to estimate the value of Buddhist temple properties. Though Fo Guang Shan lagged far behind, the article said that Tashu Village was worth NT$100,000 for each six feet square. Since the area of Fo Guang Shan was fifty acres, it was worth fifteen billion NT dollars. On reading that, I said to the abbot Hsin Ping, "I didn't know that Fo Guang Shan was worth so much. If someone were willing to buy Fo Guang Shan at even one tenth of the price, we could sell the land and give away the buildings. But who is going to buy? Can we sell it?" Shortly after, a newspaper wrote, "All Buddhist activities in Taiwan and China 'look towards' the money." I didn't know what the other temples were doing. I know that Fo Guang Shan has been founding Buddhist colleges for over thirty years. We have never charged students tuition or other fees, and we provide them with free room and board. So far, we have sixteen Buddhist colleges and six hundred students throughout the world. In addition, we have organized many free seminars for devotees in Taiwan and free Dharma lectures here and abroad. At our short-term monastic retreats, eight precepts retreats, seven-day chanting retreats, and seven-day meditation retreats we supply participants with books, clothing, and other needed gear. Despite our uncertain financial condition, we get by. So where is the money they say we "look towards"?

For the past several years, the sorry events of Chi-li Sung[3] and others have caused uproar. Because of false reports, Buddhism and relic towers became the targets of attack. Many clear-minded people realized that these events resulted from lack of proper laws and the greed of the public. It had nothing to do with orthodox Buddhism. As for the remains of the dead, they were sealed up in the towers forever. It is a pity that some people only care about the remains, without considering the caretakers' hard work. At Fo Guang Shan we provide daily chanting and special chanting services every spring and autumn to transfer merits to the departed and their relatives. In addition, we have prepared two thousand niches for the ashes of the poor of Kaohsiung County. Some reporters deviously slandered us, though they were aware of our sincerity and hard work. It made me very sad. I once lamented in a lecture that "the government was impotent, the media were not virtuous,

---

[3] A layperson who claimed to have supernatural powers to fool people.

Buddhism was innocent, and devotees could do nothing about it." For that I received great applause. This tells us that most people are basically good.

As for calling me a political monk, I rejected that from the start. None of my words or actions has to do with politics. I speak and act as a Buddhist, and I work only for the public welfare. After a while, I decided to put up with it. Many people try anything to build political connections, but they fail. Though I never sought to be political, I am a "political monk". That must mean I am able and influential. Isn't it wonderful? When I change my perspective, slander becomes sweet dew. Consequently, when I was invited to work for the Standing Committee of Central Affairs, the Committee of Revitalization of Chinese Culture, and the Committee of Overseas Affairs, I was glad to serve the public as a monk, making good affinity and volunteering to aid sentient beings.

When U.S. Vice President Al Gore visited Hsi Lai Temple on April 29, 1996, we made arrangements to show our hospitality. After certain people deliberately distorted the purpose of the visit, which was purely religious, it came to be seen as a political event. Based on the spirit of compassion, I pray that all those who intend to slander first "observe precepts, practice meditation, and cultivate wisdom to get rid of their greed, hatred, and ignorance".

When Buddhist scholar Ts'an-t'eng Chiang spoke with me several years ago in Hsinchu, Taiwan, he asked, "Though some admire you very much, why do so few want to have friendly contact with you?" He laughed when I replied, "Either it's my problem or it's his. It depends on how you see it." When we met again in Kaohsiung, he mentioned all kinds of rumors about Fo Guang Shan. I said, "Mr. Chiang, you majored in history. Your remarks should be based on fact. Why do you dwell on gossip?" He nodded his head in agreement.

"Rumors stop at the gate of the wise," they say. The *Sutra of Firm Resolve* says, "With compassion and right intention, bad karma is purged and good fortune rises. Without evil will, all evil deeds vanish." This is how the Buddha tackled rumors. "Even the Buddha was slandered." "Slander" may arise as a jealous response to our excellence. We should be grateful for slander, for it lets us examine ourselves and work out problems as we walk the path towards enlightenment.

*Good Causes and
Conditions Lead to Success*

Arriving at enlightenment while he gazed at the stars from the diamond throne under the Bodhi tree, the Buddha recognized that all the arising and ceasing in the world follows the law of causes and conditions. "Causes" are the direct inner factors that lead to the result. "Conditions" are the indirect outer facilitating factors that help produce the result. We know that the Buddha did not invent the term "causes and conditions", but they express the essence of the truths of the universe and of life that he discovered. They conform to scientific laws, and imply neither fate nor the supernatural. For over half a century of monastic life, I have reaped great benefits from the teachings. If you ask what is the most important thing I have ever learned, I reply without hesitation, "Good causes and conditions lead to success."

I was born in 1927, when Chiang Kai-shek was the commanding general in the Northern Expeditionary War. Soon followed the Sino-Japanese War and the conflict between nationalists and communists. My memory brings back one war after another, with their terrible suffering, the homes destroyed, and families separated. I thought often, "There must be some reason for the unbearable tragedy." Hearing, in a conversation between my maternal grandmother and her sister, a nun, "These are the results of the collective karma of sentient beings," "What is karma?" I asked. "The law of causality," they replied. Since renouncing worldly life, I have realized that nothing can escape the law of causes and conditions, that the cosmos is ruled by formation, existence, destruction, and non-existence, as we are ruled by birth, aging, sickness, and death, and the formation, continuance, mutability, and extinction of the mind. "Things arise out of causes and conditions; things disappear out of causes and conditions." That is the undeniable truth.

I didn't have much schooling when I was young. I learned some written words from the stories and novels I read to my bedridden mother, who corrected my mistakes. So I have the "causes and conditions" to learn words. Because our family was small, nobody cooked while she was sick. Taking initiative to cook for my family, under my mother's instructions, I had the "causes and conditions" to learn cooking. When I was very small, I was close to my grandmother, a devout Buddhist. Her chanting of the sutra and the name of the Buddha strengthened my "causes and conditions" for belief. I was greatly impressed by the elegant clothing and bearing of the many monastics in my hometown. This planted Buddhist seeds in my young mind. Unconsciously, the "causes and conditions" paved the way for my monastic life. Therefore, I can say, "Good causes and conditions lead to success."

"Causes and conditions" can be favorable or unfavorable. Timely wind and rain help plants grow. These are the favorable "causes and conditions". Frost and snow, the unfavorable "causes and conditions", also make plants stronger. In addition, there are good or evil "causes and conditions". Any "causes and conditions" that lead to success are good; any "causes and conditions" that hurt or destroy are evil. But good and evil "causes and conditions" are not absolute. One who is well taken care of by parents, and receives schooling in a prosperous society with economic growth has "good causes and conditions" to grow. One who is born to a broken family and undergoes hardships can strive and grow under the bad "causes and conditions". Looking back, I see that because I did not receive formal schooling, I cultivated myself to observe the things around me. Lacking influential relatives, I cultivated myself to love everyone and treat them equally. Lacking adequate food and clothing, I could adapt to any circumstance. Lacking a playground, I could cultivate a thoughtful character and thoroughly examine myself. These unfavorable encounters became the "causes and conditions" of my growth. As for the wars and disasters, poverty and hunger, hardships and difficulties, they became facilitating "causes and conditions".

When I studied at Ch'i-hsia Vinaya School in Nanjing, we had a shortage of teachers because of the war. Whenever a new teacher arrived, we would spread the good news. We cherished the lessons, and listened attentively. So I cultivated a good habit of listening carefully. When some mediocre teachers just wrote the material on the blackboard while saying nothing, I had the "causes and conditions" to learn to take notes. These "causes and conditions" of listening attentively and copying quickly helped me study on my own later. I realize the incredible usefulness of "causes and conditions".

I came to Taiwan during the civil conflict between the nationalists and the communists. Many of us fled, some with their families, to southern China and Taiwan. A ship that I luckily missed sank at the cost of several thousand lives, arousing great attention. Because I lacked the "causes and conditions" to be on board, I escaped death. I feel that we are moving under both favorable and unfavorable "causes and conditions", which are the invisible energy driving us everywhere.

In 1949, the Taiwan government had the mistaken idea that monks from the mainland were communist spies. In that precarious situation it was very hard to find a place to stay. I was penniless. It occurred to me that there was a Hong Kong branch of Ch'i-hsia Temple, a "Deer Park", and that a fellow monastic might give me a ticket to sail there. So I wrote for help. Before the ticket reached Taiwan, I was wrongly jailed. I was released too late, and missed my chance. Afterwards, Mr. Hung-lin Wu, Po-hsiung Wu's father and chairman of the Police-Civilian Association, vouched for me and helped me register for household residency, whereupon I changed my mind and stayed in Taiwan.

Venerable Miao Kuo, a Hakanese, offered me "causes and conditions" to stay in his temple. Although he was not a relative of mine, he gladly accepted the risk of an investigation by security agencies. Without his help, my situation would be totally different. To repay his kindness, and because of the "causes and conditions" of an engineer, Mr. Jun-te Hsieh, also a Hakanese, I have established many temples in Miaoli, Chutung, T'oufen, P'ingtung, and others for Hakanese.

After Mr. Hung-lin Wu took the risk of vouching for me, I have had good affinities with several generations of his family. Several years ago, when Mr. Wu passed away, I flew back from the Philippines to preside over his funeral. When his wife was hospitalized, I paid her several visits. In March 1998, Mr. Po-hsiung Wu succeeded me as president of B.L.I.A., R.O.C. When we went to inspect B.L.I.A. affairs, I suddenly felt the wonder of the "good causes and conditions that led to success".

After the Sino-Japanese War, I founded the *Raging Billow* monthly in Yihsing, Chiangsu. Though we printed only five hundred mimeograph copies, it became much more esteemed after the elder Venerable Ta Hsing commended it in the monthly *Sounds of Oceanic Tides*. After he arrived in Taiwan, Venerable Ta Hsing was put in charge of the Taiwan Buddhist training program in 1951. To show my appreciation for honoring our magazine, I served him as dean of studies. I can only admire the wonder of "causes and conditions", even as I brood over its vicissitudes.

During the time of the Taiwan Buddhist training program, we educated many monastics. Among them were Venerable Hsiu Ho, who was wronged and died in jail, Venerable Hsiu Yen of Ling-chuan Temple, the editor of the *Sounds of Oceanic Tides* monthly, Venerable Sheng Yin, who established Thousand-Buddha and Tzu-ming temples in Taichung, and Venerable Chen Pao, who chaired the Buddhist association in Hualien. Thanks to the "causes and conditions" I had with Venerable Ta Hsing, we trained these monastics to contribute to Buddhism in Taiwan. It was a great honor for me.

Furthermore, thanks to my "causes and conditions" with Venerable Miao Kuo he recommended me to the elders of Buddhist community, including Chen-hsiu Sung, board chairman of the Taiwan Buddhist Association, Chin-tung Lin of Pao-chueh Temple in Taichung, Chu-mu Lu of the Buddhist Association in Tainan, Ta-keng Lin of T'an-hua Buddhist Hall in Changhua, Yung-kun Tseng of the Buddhist Association in Nant'ou County, Tien-ch'un Lee and

Shih-chieh Lee, who taught at National Taiwan University, and Hsuan-ta Chang of Pei-ho High School. It was a great honor for me to be associated with them. Afterwards, they supported me when I traveled several times around the island to spread Buddhist teachings, when I advocated printing the *Chung-hua (Chinese) Buddhist Canon*, when I lectured everywhere, when I published *The Biography of Sakyamuni Buddha* and *Buddhism Today*, and at still other times. These good "causes and conditions" offset many bad "causes and conditions", so that I was able to carry out my goal of reviving Buddhism in Taiwan. Because I am thankful for the good "causes and conditions leading to success", I have vowed to provide all others with good "causes and conditions".

In around 1951, a series of earthquakes shook Hualien. I was grateful for the help of Mr. Pu-hsin Tseng of Tung-ching Temple in Hualien, a virtuous man who was always modest and sincere with me. To enable us to get along with mutual good "causes and conditions", I urged readers of *Life Monthly* to aid quake victims and to rebuild Tung-ching Temple. I also published for him the *Historical Records of Su Tung-p'o*.

When Mr. Chin-tung Lin was labeled pro-

Japanese by the government and prohibited from going abroad, I volunteered a helping hand. I suggested to the government several times that, "Mr. Lin is the best person to promote relationship with Japan." I was happy for him when the ban was lifted and he was allowed to visit Japan.

Once, when a Ma-chu[1] pilgrims group from Changhua visited a Ma-chu temple in Peikang, I was invited by Mr. Ta-keng Lin to come by on a tricycle and have a look. This gave me a deep understanding of folk religion in Taiwan. To repay his hospitality, I invited him to serve as vice president of Fu-shan Buddhist College in our Fu-shan Temple, Changhua. I hoped that our good "causes and conditions" would help promote Buddhism in the Changhua area.

Subsequently, many monastics provided me with good "causes and conditions" to spread Buddhist teachings. Among them were Venerable Yuan Jung of Tung-shan Temple, Pintung; Venerable Chih Tao of Ching-chueh Temple, Miaoli; Venerable Te Hsi of Shen-chai Hall; Venerable Miao Pen of Pi-lu Temple, Houli; Venerables Shan Ting and Hui Ting of Chao-yuan Temple, Meinung; and Venerable Wen Chih of Bodhi Hall, Panch'iao. I

---

[1] A female folk deity.

worked hard to repay their kindness, writing and mailing them books and magazines.

In 1952, I got a written invitation from upasaka[2] T'eng Ma to preach in Ilan, and then was invited in person by Mr. Chueh-ho Lee to settle in Ilan. I gladly agreed. When T'eng Ma died at Kangshan forty-six years later, in 1998, over eighty years old, I went to Kangshan to make incense offering and pray for him, to show my thanks for his giving me a good "cause" to go to Ilan. I instructed my disciples Man Ching and Yung Nen to take good care of his funeral arrangements and to place his remains in our cemetery garden.

Thirty years ago, when I preached in the area around K'en-ting Park, I was invited by the Lien-hai chanting group to preside over its inauguration ceremony. This year, when I was invited to preside over a chanting service for Tung-hai Temple, I learned that there were now several dozen temples in the area. I recalled the words of Buddhist scripture: the seed of a nyagrodha[3] tree is small, but

---

[2] A householder who practices Buddhism at home without being a monastic.

[3] Planted in India and Sri Lanka, nyagrodha trees can grow as tall as ten or fifteen meters. The branches and leaves are vast, but the seeds are very small. In Buddhist scripture, the seed of the nyagrodha tree is usually compared to a small cause leading to a great consequence.

the mature tree is vast and shades many passersby. This shows how a small "cause" can bear great fruit. Those who plant do not necessarily enjoy the result themselves, but they take delight in the shade that benefits the public.

When I first went to Ilan, I had been only a receiver of causes and conditions. I thought, "What 'causes and conditions' can I give to others?" So whenever I got some money, I bought *Life Monthly, Bodhi Tree Monthly,* and Buddhist books, and distributed them to temples, shops, devotees, and young people. These "causes and conditions" promoted the study of Buddhist teachings in Ilan, and the setting up of chanting groups in T'ou-ch'eng and Lotung. Unexpectedly, Venerable Chueh Yi of Yuang-ming Temple provided me with a hut for writing and practice. I got to know Mr. T'ieh-cheng Fang, Mr. Chueh-ho Lee's son-in-law, while circulating Buddhist books. Owing to these "causes and conditions", Mr. Chueh-ho Lee followed me into monasticism at a ripe age, and his daughter, Tzu Chuang, and his grandsons, Hui Lung and Hui Chuan, also followed me into monasticism, and now perform important tasks at Fo Guang Shan.

The "causes and conditions" in Ilan brought many talented youths to help me launch Buddhist enterprises. Some became monastics who built Fo Guang Shan with me. Among the outstanding laity are professor Shih-yen Cheng, who benefits many with his professional knowledge of psychology, and Tzu-bin Yang, Chao Chang, Kang-ch'ui Chang, and Ching-chih Lin, who work hard for Fo Guang University and other enterprises. These good "causes and conditions" operate together, like the beads of a string, meanwhile growing ever larger like rolling snowballs. Remote Ilan has been transformed into the cradle of Buddhism in Taiwan. The history of our work in Ilan is amazing.

When you benefit others with just a sentence of Buddhist teaching, or when you show concern for them, you pass on "causes and conditions". Even a sincere smile or a simple book about Buddhism provides people with good "causes and conditions". In my many years of getting along with fellow monastics and devotees I have felt the importance of cherishing relationships with old and new friends. The only thing that can forever sustain good "causes and conditions" is the social bridge built of sentiment and love through practice and cultivation.

In 1955, a group of monastics that included Venerable Nan T'ing, Ven. Chu Yun, and me, organized an around-the-island preaching group to support the *Chinese Buddhist Canon.* For an entire month, we went everywhere by ox-cart, tricycle, train, car, ship, warship, and airplane. Wherever we went, we were greeted with firecrackers and flowers, gongs and drums. Local temples brought out their deities in golden sedan chairs. Loudspeakers made the mood jolly. People came down from the stage to mingle joyfully with the audience. After that successful tour, I led many more, accompanied by students and young adults. We were always warmly welcomed. Some say that I provide the "causes and conditions" to help promote Buddhism in Taiwan, but I think the people of Taiwan provide me with good "causes and conditions" to revive Buddhism.

Reflecting on the past four decades, I realize that Buddhist teachings have spread quickly everywhere because of favorable "causes and conditions". For example, the radio program *The Voice of Buddhism* enabled many people to have "causes and conditions" to learn Buddhism. Thanks to the "causes and conditions" of Yi-chi Chan, who provided college scholarships for studying Buddhism, many colleges set up Buddhist clubs, one after the other. Thanks to the "causes and conditions" of Ching-chou Chu and Shao-chi Chang, who published Buddhist scriptures, many readers could cultivate wisdom as deep as the ocean. Thanks to the "causes and conditions" of Venerable Pai Sheng and others, who organized ordination ceremonies for many years, the number of monastics has grown. Thanks to the "causes and conditions" of Fo Guang Shan, which founded Buddhist colleges, the level of Buddhist education has risen.

The Buddha was born to this world for great "causes and conditions", i.e., to teach sentient beings how to attain enlightenment. One thousand years ago, thanks to the "causes and conditions" of Emperor Ming of the Eastern Han dynasty [25-220 C.E.], who dreamed of a golden figure, Buddhism was spread to the East. But Buddhism also came as a reward to people whose merit and virtue entitled them to the teachings. At the end of the twentieth century, Buddhism was being spread to the West. These will be wonderful "causes and conditions" for the Buddha's light to shine everywhere and for the Dharma water to flow forever.

When I inaugurated our American temple, China and the United States were on good terms. Many poor Chinese students went to the United

States to further their studies. Mr. Hsiao-jui P'an and I set up the Hsi Lai Scholarship program to endow each of them with between US$3,000 and US$10,000, to provide good "causes and conditions". We supported the famous writer Ah Ch'eng, Ling-ling Shih, Chen-yang Kuo, and others. Journalist Ta-chung Pu and musician Hui-shan Chen also got their scholarships from us. Mr. Tan Wang rejected other offers but accepted ours. It is clear that the scholarship program of Hsi Lai University is a quite pure and benevolent "cause and condition".

When a famous writer, Pei Tao, asked for help to publish a literary journal, I gladly provided him with financial "causes and conditions". When Dr. Hui-wen von Groeling-Che of Hamburg University convened a conference of the Association of Chinese Scholars in Europe (ACSE) in Paris in 1995, she asked us to pay room and board and transportation for all participants. I felt it was a great honor to provide international Chinese scholars with some good "causes and conditions", so I gladly pledged to help. All previous World Fellowship of Buddhists conferences were convened in Asian countries, though not in Taiwan. But under the auspices of Fo Guang Shan, the 16th conference was held at Hsi Lai Temple in Los Angeles in 1988, the 18th was at Fo Guang Shan in Taiwan in 1992, and the 20th at Nan Tien Temple in Australia in 1998. It was expensive to host these conferences, but I treasured the rare "causes and conditions" that allowed me to make my best effort to promote international Buddhism.

I feel deeply that as long as there are "causes and conditions", there is hope; as long as there are "causes and conditions", there is comfort; as long as there are "causes and conditions", there is success. It's so wonderful to have good "causes and conditions". Therefore, I always remind myself to feel gratitude for past "causes and conditions", to seize the present "causes and conditions", and to cultivate future "causes and conditions". That is the way I can open up a bright life for others and myself.

In order to contribute some "causes and conditions" for Buddhist research, I invited scholars from China and Taiwan to publish *Chinese Buddhist Canon Treasure*. To spread Bodhi seeds everywhere, I have been busy traveling at home and abroad, delivering Buddhist lectures that confer some causes and conditions on others. To propagate Buddhism on television, I have made programs of five minutes, a half hour, an hour, and longer. During the past three decades, we have expanded our broadcast network from one television station to three, from wireless to cable, and even to our own Buddha's Light Satellite Television station, so that our growing audience can have some good "causes and conditions". We have organized many seminars to provide good "causes and conditions" to sponsors, devotees, ladies, male volunteers, youth, and monastics. Though Fo Guang Shan is only about thirty years old, we have already convened over thirty international conferences throughout the world, to provide intellectuals some "causes and conditions" of Buddhism. Though established only in 1992, Buddha's Light International Association has organized over seven thousand public activities at home and abroad to provide people with causes and conditions to purify their minds.

For forty years, I have worked hard to conduct refuge ceremonies and five precepts retreats and to organize short-term monastic retreats to provide good "causes and conditions" for people. My goals are these: to found universities for those who should be connected with Buddhism through the "causes and conditions" of universities; to found

Buddha's Light International Association for those who should be connected with Buddhism through the "causes and conditions" of Buddha's Light International Association; to build temples for those who should be connected with Buddhism through the "causes and conditions" of temples; to build Buddhist colleges for those who should be connected with Buddhism through the "causes and conditions" of Buddhist colleges; to build art galleries for those who should be connected with Buddhism through the "causes and conditions" of art galleries; to establish young adults divisions for those who should be connected with Buddhism through the "causes and conditions" of young adults divisions; to organize study groups for those who should be connected with Buddhism through the "causes and conditions" of study groups.

Buddhism advocates the ideal of integration of causes and conditions. As we know, causes and conditions are interrelated. There is no way for them to exist alone. Good causes and conditions lead to success. Those who understand the interrelationship of causes and conditions can enjoy endless achievements.

A Job Without Pay

In May 1998, Ms. Shu-chih Fan of the Dhammakaya Foundation in Thailand spent a couple of days at Fo Guang Shan. She had just escorted the Buddha's tooth relic to Taiwan in the company of Mr. Phillip Thiarry, president of the World Fellowship of Buddhist Youth. While there she said to me, "I have been very happy working in the Dhammakaya Foundation for ten years. Happy because I'm not working for money, but rather doing the job without pay." Though I understood what she meant, I asked, "What is good about doing a job without pay?" She replied, "If I were working for money, I would be sensitive about how much money I could earn, how many holidays I could have, and how much I can accomplish. There would be no fun at all. But because I am doing my job without pay, the conscientious responsibility and mission of my life, I must perform it well. Therefore, I feel happier doing it without pay." How wonderful! She is consequently often so busy she forgets to eat, and cheerfully forgets her troubles. After many years of such work she has reached the state of mindfulness. This may be the same Dharma joy felt by all disciples and devotees of Fo Guang Shan through their belief.

Many people ask curiously why many senior monastics are willing to devote their lives to Fo Guang Shan for decades without regret? If we think about it, we grasp that they do not ask for special privileges because they simply wish to help spread Buddhism everywhere. Among others, Hsin Ping worked in the Chung-hua Printing Company, Tzu Chuang worked at Lanyang Girls' High School, Tzu Hui worked at a tax office, Tzu Jung worked at a pharmacy, Hsin Ting worked at the post office, Hui-hua Hsiao worked in the Telecommunications Bureau. Thirty years ago, they resigned their high paying jobs to devote their time and effort to spreading Buddhist teachings. Every month, they received only an allowance of NT\$20. But they have been more influential than those who work for pay, because they think little of money, and prosper from the Dharma joy of spreading the teachings.

When Professor Yu, who was attending a Buddhist conference at Hsi Lai Temple, saw the monastics happily at work from morning till night, he sighed that he could never find such an assistant, and wondered why so many devoted themselves wholeheartedly to me? I said, "Because I regard Dharma propagation as my family obligation, and benefiting sentient beings as my enterprise. I have been perfectly willing to do 'a job without pay'." For many years I have considered myself to be just one of the group. I never ordered others to work. Therefore, everyone is more ready to do the "job without pay".

I have been receiving free medical and dental services from Dr. Yen Chang, my heart surgeon at Veteran's Hospital, Dr. Jen-yee Shen, M.D. and Ph.D., a dermatologist, Dr. Garlan G. Lo, M.D., an ophthalmologist, and Dr. Steve J.H. Lee, a dentist in Los Angeles. They have treated my disciples and me patiently and sincerely, like family.

"A job without 'pay' makes one energetic at work," said Chin-pao Huang, head of B.L.I.A. Young Adults Subdivision, Taipei. For many years I have seen her work with a group of young staff at P'u-men Temple, Taipei Temple, and even at Fo Guang Shan during holidays. It occurs to me that many admirable volunteers devote themselves to the temples without asking anything in return. Mr. Chueh-ho Lee handled general affairs at Lei-yin Temple, Ilan for over twenty years. Subsequently, he followed me into monasticism and was renamed Hui Ho. The assemblyman Po-fen Chen devoted himself to the construction of the cemetery garden at Fo Guang Shan and to Fo Guang University. In addition, there were Sung-nien Lin, Ai Kuo, Tzu-ju chen, and Shu-jen Lu-Hung, volunteers at Lei-yin Temple in the early years, as well as Yueh-kuei Su, Hung-hui Lee, Teng-jui Yu, and Hui-yin Hsu in Taipei, Ts'ui-ying Sun and Feng-ying Lee in Keelung, Yu-ch'eng Shen, Chia-lung Hung, and Yi-ming Lai in central Taiwan, Chin-fei Tseng, Shun-chang Chen, Hui-chen Yueh, Ying-fang Hsiao, and others.

There are overseas volunteers, such as Carl Tsai of Toronto, Sophia Hsieh of Vancouver, Wen-Luan Loh of Boston, Lydia Chao of Houston, Jim Chen of Los Angeles, Hoo-Pang Ngiam of Hong Kong, Datin Tan Swee Lai of Malaysia, Nishihara of Tokyo, Henry You and Robert Liao of Sydney, Chao-ming Liu of Brisbane, Francois Kan of Paris, Sheng-kai Chang of Sao Paulo, and Rene Gienjuina of South Africa. Most notably, Mr. Po-hsiung Wu, the presidential advisor, said publicly that he was a volunteer at Taipei Temple. It touched me that he was going to put aside politics and focus on Buddhism.

For years, I have come often to Taipei Temple. Usually, I see many volunteers busy in the early morning, cleaning windows and restrooms, mopping floors, making tea, and so on. After that, some go to offices by bus, and some stay to serve at our temple. Many of them are wealthy and revered, and are attended by servants at home. But when they come to Taipei Temple, they volunteer to work. If they paid attention to their treatment, instead of to practice and cultivation, how could they be enthusiastic? Therefore, I always say, "Honors belong to the Buddha; achievements belong to the multitude."

Fo Guang Shan has over one thousand monastics and staff. They work throughout the year without a holiday. Some cook in the kitchen, some guide tours, some take care of the Buddha Hall, and some work in the educational and cultural departments. In addition, they have to join morning and evening chanting sessions, study Buddhism, and seize every moment to work and practice. But they declare "the job without pay" makes their lives happy and meaningful. In doing "a job without pay", there is dignity, sincerity of dedication, joy of aspiration, and endless worth.

Students at Fo Guang Shan's Buddhist colleges have to work for the Temple one hour each afternoon during summer, winter, and New Year vacations. Sometimes, even the day before examinations they are still at work, cooking, serving in the dining hall, working in the Buddha Hall, and receiving visitors. Yet they practice and cultivate wholeheartedly. I often advised teachers, "It's important for students to focus on study. They should have more time to prepare for examinations." But the students replied, "We practice and cultivate here. We should do more to help spread Buddhist teachings. Fo Guang Shan is a place to cultivate our Buddha nature. We want to pass the examination by the Buddha." I can say that "a job without pay" scores one hundred.

In the past, the famed Ta-hsien Temple in Tainan accommodated over three hundred monastics. According to their rule, monastics had to toil for the Temple for fifteen years before getting their own living quarters. Monastics at Fo Guang Shan, however, do not have to worry about room and board. They enjoy the Dharma joy of devoting themselves. Tzu Chuang lived on a small ranch when building Hsi Lai Temple. Man Che lived in a garage when she first went to Germany. Without the merits and virtues of the Buddhas and Bodhisattvas, how else would they be so willing? Without a sense of mission, how would monastics and laity work together to build temples, Buddha's

Light purelands, throughout the world? Clearly, "a job without pay" is much more rewarding. Those doing "a job without pay" are the wealthiest in the world.

Shih-liang Huang and Hsiu-lan Lin have been my devotees since Ilan, forty-five years ago. Not yet married, they asked me to let them enter monasticism. Without a temple, I could not provide them with Buddhist education. So I persuaded them to cultivate as lay people. Though they later married, they agreed not to be bound by the married life and not to have children. When I started building Fo Guang Shan, they left their business to work with me. For twenty years, Mr. Huang has managed the water and electricity, while Mrs. Huang has served the multitude. They have never demanded payment, but instead donated the rent from their house to Buddhist enterprises. It's easy enough to start a difficult undertaking, but it's hard to keep it up. It's easy to do "a job without pay", but hard to be happy decade after decade.

When industrial and commercial workers in Taipei went on strike for a pay raise, it was quite a shock to Taiwan. I calmly told an assembly of almost a thousand staff members at Fo Guang

Shan, "You can demonstrate for a raise before the Buddha Hall or the Pilgrims' Lodge." Unexpectedly, an old man who swept the grounds rose to speak, "We are not here for pay, but for happiness and merit." I asked him, "What is the fun of working at Fo Guang Shan?" He said, "Monastics respect us and address us kindly with smiles, and show concern for us. Working here, we are full of dignity and joy. This is the unsurpassed 'pay'. Why should we demonstrate for a raise of 'pay'?"

It's fun to do "a job without pay". Throughout my life, I have never had a summer or winter vacation, a weekend off, New Year holidays, or any other holiday, and I have never demanded any special privilege. I never got my salary when I was the principal of the White Tower Elementary School in China. I told my Dharma brother, "Please divide my salary into two parts, one for the temple and the other for my mother."

In my ten years of monastic training, I formed a habit of not spending money. "A job with pay" was "a job without pay" for me. After arriving in Taiwan, when I was dean of studies of the Taiwan Buddhist training program, my monthly allowance was NT$50. I always used the money to subscribe to Buddhist journals or to buy books for students.

When I served for decades in the Buddhist chanting group in Ilan, I used my monthly allowance of NT$300 to buy equipment for Dharma propagation and to encourage young people to teach everywhere. During that time, all the railway stationmasters from Suao to Juifang took refuge in the Triple Gem. Mr. Wen-ping Chang of Ilan station never charged us for fare because he thought we had contributed much to Buddhism. That let me save even more for Dharma propagation. I am thankful whenever I think about him. In addition to Dharma propagation, I bought souvenirs and necklaces with sauvastika for making affinity with young people. Because Christianity was popular, many people wore a cross around their neck. But the sight of those lovely young people wearing sauvastika necklaces attracted great attention. Whenever I think of it, I am so happy that those young people were brave enough to wear the necklace when society was conformist and Buddhism was largely suppressed.

When we began building Fo Guang Shan, pilgrims came from Taipei every weekend. I usually conducted refuge ceremony for them during morning chanting session. In return, they offered me red envelopes with money. Though unaccustomed to such payments, I accepted them to buy desks, chairs, and cushions for the multitude. For decades, I have been delighted to see devotees use them, for they are emblems of my sincerity.

I have never accepted money when I am invited to lecture at colleges and universities. But when I am invited to lecture at businesses or factories, I accept their money in order to avoid a scene, and consider ways to spend it on the multitude. I was one of the lecturers in the training program for government employees in Taiwan, one of the professors for the youth trained in the Ch'eng-kung-ling (Ridge of Success), and a professor at Chinese Culture University and Tung-hai University. I accepted their money only to buy books for the Fo Guang Shan branch libraries. Though many readers are unaware of my benevolent work, the joy I take in seeing them read my books is beyond measure.

For decades I have been the unpaid supervisor of the Chinese Buddhist Association, and the director and standing director of many of the Association's Taiwanese divisions. Even as the standing counsel or advisory committee member, I did not receive any pay. I have presided at inaugurations and ribbon-cuttings for many temples without asking for payment. In doing a lot of "jobs without pay", I have made a lot of good affinity.

Like other aspirants, I am glad to be a volunteer for society. I was the counsel of the Mongolian-Tibetan Committee, a member of the Overseas Chinese Affairs Committee, and a lecturer to prisoners for the Ministry of Justice. I was happy to do these "jobs without pay". I believe that serving others is what one should do. It is as natural as breathing. Sometimes, during Chinese New Year or Mid-autumn Festival, I received gifts from former presidents Ching-kuo Chiang and Teng-hui Lee. To show courtesy, I always repaid them with Buddhist books.

In addition to performing jobs without pay, I wrote for *Buddhism Today*, *Life Monthly*, *Universal Gate*, and *Awakening the World*. I even paid for draft paper, letter paper, postage, and transportation. I have founded Buddhist colleges for over thirty years and assumed the unpaid jobs of president and teacher. Not only do I not charge tuition, I provide free room and board, clothes, and other essentials. It is very rewarding to see so many people provided with good causes and conditions to learn Buddhism, and to see that many young people are well educated.

Many branches of Fo Guang Shan have founded Chinese schools and classes for talented people. Though I hoped that classes could be free, my disciples told me they had to pay teachers salaries. While we Buddhists follow the law of causality, the rules for non-Buddhists are both to carry out obligations and to enjoy rights. So, following the times, I agree with my disciples that to get what you want you must give what others need.

"A job without pay" is not necessarily bad, and a job with pay is not necessarily good. From my point of view, creating a bright future for Buddhism requires providing jobs so that people can carry out their duties and enjoy their rights, and not insisting that they volunteer indefinitely.

I have known many retired volunteers who have no family to support, so that they are able to devote their time and effort wholeheartedly. I wondered, "How many enterprises can be run by volunteers this way? Temples should offer their staff reasonable pay." Therefore, since establishing P'u-men High School, Fo Guang Publishing House, *Universal Gate* Magazine, Fo Guang University, and others, I have paid my staffs a salary.

Employees can pay their living expenses and still work for Dharma propagation wholeheartedly. Even when one does not have to earn a living for his family, he can be rich with Buddhist teachings in his mind and yet not reject the pay. "Have and have-not are just two sides of one coin." Without attachment and rejection, the life of the middle way is the most wonderful state of practice.

In addition, Buddhist temples should provide channels of development for learned and professional volunteers, who are willing to contribute without asking any privileges. Mr. Cheng-yi Kao, after retiring as a senior engineer from the Ministry of Economics, turned down an invitation with high pay to direct construction of the Three Gorges dam on the Yangtze River in China. He preferred to devote his entire energy and thought to the construction of Fo Guang University. Mr. Tzu-lang Yu, of Tung-yuan Electrical Engineering Company in Chiayi, quit his job as supervisor of the Salvation Corps in Chiayi, but volunteered to supervise the construction of Nan Hua University. Ms. Yueh-ying Chen-Yu, advisor of national policy in Kaohsiung, also spoke for Fo Guang Shan. I joked to her, "You act more like the abbot of Fo Guang Shan." She smiled. Lawyers

Chien-chung Su in Taipei and Ying-kuei Su in Kaohsiung, and vocational college teacher Ch'ao-p'ai Chen have protected Fo Guang Shan as if their lives were at stake. It is very hard to find such devoted people even at a high salary. Deeply moved, I show more reverence to them. From them I realize that "doing a job without pay" is truly much more rewarding.

All teachers and staff of P'u-men High School are paid like those at public high schools. Monastics of Fo Guang Shan receive a monthly allowance of NT$300. Once, a teacher at P'u-men High School used up his salary and said to a monastic, "Could you lend me your allowance?" We can see from this example that those who earn money do not necessarily own much and those who "work without pay" do not necessarily own nothing.

In February 1998, I conducted the international full ordination ceremony in Bodhgaya. Many highly cultivated monastics from over twenty countries were invited for teaching, instruction, and discipline. None of them demanded any special treatment. How precious it is that monastics work hard to propagate teachings and benefit sentient beings without being concerned about gain and loss! President Chang of B.L.I.A., Brazil, not only donated his house to serve as our temple, but also bought land to build the biggest temple in South America, and is planning to build a Buddhist college. President Chao of I.B.P.S., Houston, bought land for a temple and raised funds for construction. It is splendid that so many lay people devote their money and effort to propagating Buddhism and benefiting sentient beings. Compared to those who worry about gain and loss, isn't the merit of non-attachment more perfect? Having is finite and exhaustible, but not-having is infinite and inexhaustible. "A job without pay" opens up a wider world for us.

I have never asked for "a job with pay". Moreover, since I began building Fo Guang Shan, I have enjoyed "considering nothing as having". We were poor, not even knowing if we would eat tomorrow. Every day was hard, but we got by. It reminds me of an ancient verse, "There is hope in a desperate situation." Always I have felt the Dharma joy and been full of hope. According to the *Heart Sutra,* "As there is nothing to attain, a Bodhisattva that relies on the Prajna Paramita has neither worry nor obstruction. Without worry and obstruction, there is no fear. Absent confusion and day-dreaming, one reaches nirvana." It's true. Therefore, though "a job without pay" seems impoverished, it is a perfectly willing job to make affinity with others. Though "a job without pay" seems worthless, it is a real job to gain merit and Dharma fortune.

When we affirm the equal importance of obligations and privileges, let us also praise "the job without pay". It is both the job of Buddhists and a living philosophy that lets us possess the endless world and endless benefit.

*Numerous Experiences
of Life and Death*

Several times have I come close to dying. In the chaos of the civil conflict both communists and nationalists treated me as a spy. I was jailed several times and once nearly shot. At twenty-eight, I was advised to amputate my leg to save my life. But thanks to the blessing of the Buddha, I unexpectedly recovered. At fifty-four, I was told by my doctor that I would die in two months. I survived by keeping busy at my job. In 1995, nearing seventy, I underwent heart surgery with a fifty percent chance of success. I accepted it calmly because I know we all have to endure "numerous experiences of life and death". We have to face the facts of life and death, of good and evil. Afterwards, I reflected somberly on the "numerous experiences of life and death" that are the story of my life.

In my childhood, my impoverished parents took no special care of me, but I always treasure my affection for them. When I came into the monastic life, I thought often of my parents and maternal grandmother. It was hard not to think of them. And I was always deeply concerned for my brothers and sister and other relatives. Whenever I heard news from my hometown, and also when my sister brought me two pairs of shoes, my serene mind was shaken. When a message came from my first master (he wished to be my master when I was a month old), saying how he missed me, and again when a classmate wrote to me, I yearned to be home. Many times I wanted to visit my mother and my relations, but the monastery rules prohibited it. After "numerous experiences of life and death", I was no longer impeded by such defiled thinking and private feelings, and could immerse myself in the boundless ocean of the Dharma.

I imagined I could transcend the world, but my heart was constantly shaken by my zeal to love and protect Buddhism. I thought, "Who, if not I, will revive Buddhism and save sentient beings?" I overflowed with righteousness. When I saw so many injustices in society and country, and observed the incompetence of some important Buddhists, I would wake at midnight with a passionate desire to revive Buddhism. After continually wrestling with this sentiment, I realized that it was useless to be merely ardent and sincere. I had to cultivate myself intensely, so that I might be able to seize some future chance. One who is well trained needs not fear failure. Therefore, I rose above merely loving Buddhism, and dedicated myself to hard work. And then I felt the bondage of "numerous experiences of life and death" fall away.

As a beginning student, I was illiterate and ignorant. I had a poor memory and lagged behind my class. Slowly, I learned to read, analyze, and think quickly. I became a top student. The mind, like the snake, grows large after several times shedding its skin ("numerous experiences of life and death"). During the war we suffered privation and hardship. Whenever I changed schools, I had to let go of my old teachers and classmates and put up with new ones. By that continual process I learned to face impermanence with a serene mind. I realize now that I could not have succeeded in my study and practice without "numerous experiences of life and death".

Sitting in the meditation hall can be unbearable to the untrained. The mind leaps from branch to branch like the monkey mind. The legs grow numb. If we would chant the name of the Buddha in the right state of mind, we must conquer our demons through the trial of "numerous experiences of life and death". After that we forget self-existence.

When the Japanese invaded our country I was just a child. At ten, I wanted to join the guerrillas. After full ordination as a monk, I wanted to be a monastic policeman protecting Buddhism and the monasteries. And I wanted to start up secular Buddhist enterprises, such as farming, mining, ceramics, schools, hospitals, newspapers, cinema, etc. I felt that monastics should be industrious and not parasites. Seeing farmland, I thought of Buddhist seeds to be planted and fruit to be picked. In factory smoke I saw the Buddha's teachings. I was planning night and day, as if driven by karmic energy. I successfully managed White Tower Elementary School, Ta-chueh Farm, Yi-hua Stationery, Hua-ts'ang Pure Water, Hua-ts'ang Elementary School, Hua-ts'ang Fabrics, and more. Regrettably, they all vanished in the defeat of the nationalist army. Then my mind went blank and I did not know what to do.

After the nightmare of separatist warlords came the eight-year war against Japan. Before the dead were buried, the war of nationalists and communists broke out. Everywhere, people suffered extreme privation. To help our wounded soldiers, I joined the Sangha Relief Group on the battlefield. But after "numerous experiences of life and death" our efforts failed, and we were regrettably compelled to disband upon arrival in Taiwan.

My ten years at Buddhist colleges were seared by poverty. Being unable to pay postage, I could only pocket the letters I wrote to my mother. At length, I found no less than ten in my pocket. I wore the clothing and shoes of departed monks. The shoes I mended with paper. The holes in the clothes seemed to express the monastics' determination to learn the teachings and practice through "numerous experiences of life and death".

When I fled Chiaoshan for Nanjing and Taiwan, I had to give away my books and clothes. After arriving at the port of Keelung, we trekked Taiwan from north to south and back again, stared at by barefoot people. Following custom, we discarded our shoes and donned broad-brimmed rain hats. Later, when Venerable Chu Yun came to Taiwan from P'u-t'o Shan, I gave him my only garment. For years afterwards, I wore only *tuan-kua*.[1] When I finally got some money, I bought fabric, dyed it, and made myself a new garment. Feeling as if I had recovered something lost, I sensed that the past could be restored. I saw that "numerous experiences of life and death" lay right before me. Why, then, do we think we must wait for a later time to experience transmigration to

---

[1] The clothes worn inside the garment.

another place?

For a long time I went hungry, uncertain of my next meal. After going to Sun Moon Lake for Dharma preaching, I had to sell the Parker pen I had just been given to pay for a return ticket. Often I couldn't afford a bus ticket, and had to walk from Taipei to Wanhua to edit the magazine. When I worked on formatting at the printing company, I appeased my hunger with water because I couldn't afford a piece of bread. But achieving my life of wisdom was well worth suffering "numerous experiences of life and death".

If we cannot put up with slander, malicious acts arising from hate and jealousy, cold glares, and defiant stares, and if we are not firm in our minds, we cannot liberate ourselves from the defilements of "numerous experiences of life and death". If we drown in the ocean of ignorance, we shall suffer endlessly the cycle of birth and death.

I hated myself for not being gifted and for my poor education. I feared that I lacked good causes and conditions, and that I had not the right upbringing to glorify the Buddhist tradition. I was angry that the world was hardnosed and unjust, that society was lawless, and that troubles at home and abroad caused so much hardship and suffering. And when I examined myself, I was ashamed of my deficiency of merit, fortune, practice and cultivation, social standing, and ability. But I determined to improve myself. If I did not change, did not liberate myself from the troubling "numerous experiences of life and death", how would I enjoy peace and steadiness in body and mind?

When I came to the dazzling bustling city, whose monastics practice with matching intensity, I grew depressed. An introvert struggling with "numerous experiences of life and death", I forced myself to embrace the multitude. As a monk at Ch'i-hsia Temple, I declined appointment as abbot, preferring to devote myself to teaching. But Buddhism was not yet thriving in Taiwan, and there were not enough students to teach. There was only the tedium of writing magazine articles. I had to sit chained to a desk, racking my brain for ideas. Finishing an article was like trans-migrating to another life. But I was viewed as lazy and unproductive. I feared I would fall short of my goal, but I did not care for com-promise. My thoughts came in waves, like the tide of "numerous experiences of life and death". Finally, I accepted a compromise. I would serve the multitude in the temple by day, but my nights I would devote to my writing. Afterwards, I began lecturing lay people while building temples for the monastics. This life was not entirely satisfactory, and doubts lingered like "numerous experiences of life and death". But circumstances left me no choice. Since founding Fo Guang Shan, I have advocated "to educate the talented through education, to propagate Buddhism through cultural activities, to benefit society through charity, and to purify people's minds through practice together". I have never repented this decision, and I never shall. I am thankful for the Triple Gem, heavenly guardians, and all devotees who have protected, assisted, and respected me. Without them, how can I liberate myself from the defilements and delusions of "numerous experiences of life and death", and carry out the ideal to "let the Buddha's light shine throughout the three thousand great chiliocosms, and let the Dharma water flow through six continents"?

Travel overseas to teach may seem fantastic. In reality, I am often cooped up on a ten-hour flight, unable to move. On arrival, I feel drained. Often I fly from tropic to frost, enduring changes of climate, time, custom, and food. Then I face a tiring round of lectures, visitors, seminars, and photo sessions. My hotel suite serves as guest room, dining room, conference room, and telephone booth. Different kinds of people require different treatment. Unusual problems arise. Whenever I go abroad, it's like "numerous experiences of life and death". And I have to do it several times a year.

Some people are bright enough to grasp the teachings at once, but I had to study them again and again. Some people reach their goals swiftly and without a hitch, but I have to try over and over. Where there is a will, there is a way. Through my determination to go through "numerous experiences of life and death", I press on until I succeed.

We have grown from one college to sixteen, from twenty students to nearly two thousand. To follow causes and conditions we have improved our educational system, brought in new teachers, enhanced our curriculum, and adopted new teaching methods. Though our Buddhist education has only thirty-four years of history, it has "numerous experiences of life and death".

In the course of publishing more than a thousand issues of *Awakening the World* we have seen many changes. We moved our offices at least ten times. Our magazine went through several style changes. Circulation exploded from two thousand to four hundred thousand. We know that magazine publishing is a risky business, but ours flourishes because we have braced ourselves for "numerous experiences of life and death". And we always come up with new ideas.

Composing just a short *Ode to the Triple Gem* forces me to think hard, going through "experiences of life and death". If I had not spent forty years thinking, would there be singing of the Triple Gem at all Buddhist gatherings today?

Starting with Lei-yin and Shou-shan temples, we now have some two hundred temples on six continents. Establishing temples takes money, manpower, and hard work. I can say that all our achievements come from "numerous experiences of life and death".

Fighting nature seems to offer "numerous experiences of life and death". Government officials delayed the registration of Fo Guang Shan for ten years, and permits for some buildings arrived only after the thirtieth anniversary. Floods toppled the Release Pool again and again; typhoons brought down the retaining walls. I worried when the rainy season came, and my disciples and I spent whole days inspecting the grounds. On the first day of our first Buddhist summer camp for college students, the water pump broke down. Watching the repairman, I vowed before the Buddha, "I will change my blood into water to supply the camp, if I have to." After the pump was fixed, I was not satisfied until I had crossed the woods and climbed the tower to touch the flowing water. Hearing the beat of the wooden board announcing the morning chanting, I realized that I hadn't slept all night. It seemed I had undergone a nightmare with "numerous experiences of life and death".

When I organized activities, I worried that no one would sign up. When I organized Dharma functions, I worried about overlooked details. When I hosted Dharma lectures, I worried about rain. When I published magazines, I worried about deadlines. Everything demands thorough planning. We must be determined to do the job right; to properly manage people, places, and resources; and to have the right attitude for the job and for the "numerous experiences of life and death" that come with it. Without determination, how can we do our jobs well?

When I was planning Hsi Lai Temple, we walked from door to door, in the rain, to discuss our plans with our neighbors. Only after six public hearings and more than a hundred negotiating sessions were we allowed to begin building. Over the next ten years, our neighbors gradually accepted us. Without the training of "numerous experiences of life and death", how could we have had the toughness to build the biggest Buddhist temple in North America? Without "numerous experiences of life and death", how could we have won the respect of westerners? It is a shame that in graciously hosting Vice President Al Gore, we were subjected to an investigation of political contributions. Yi Chu and Man Ho were repeatedly questioned, and the temple had to pay expensive legal fees, because our hospitality was mis-represented. All the good things we have done in America were obscured by a single political incident. But though the "numerous experiences of life and death" were hard to bear, we coped magnificently.

After we were given land to build Nan Tien Temple in Australia and Nan Hua Temple in South Africa, we had to negotiate with mayors and councilmen, and plan with architects and engineers. Tzu Chuang, Tzu Jung, and I made several ten-hour flights to inspect progress. Because we were determined to face "numerous experiences of life and death", we succeeded in building the largest Buddhist temple in the Southern Hemisphere, and we cast the light of hope on Africa, the Dark Continent.

As a child, being scolded, punished, and even mistreated by my teachers made me sad. But only in the beginning, until I learned to bear it. Growing up required "numerous experiences of life and death". When I started accepting devotees and disciples, many people envied me for having so many. But how many of my followers understand me? It takes many years to educate a devotee. Without the power of "numerous experiences of life and death", how can the disciple gain a firm faith in Buddhism? To educate, I must be compassionate and inspiring. Without the patience acquired through "numerous experiences of life and death", how can my disciples be well educated? Some disciples who misunderstood me complained, "You tend to believe everything you have been told." "You don't understand me." "You are not fair." The fact is I treat all disciples alike. But I accept their complaints in the spirit of "numerous experiences of life and death". How else could I lead them to practice?

Hardship, honor, frustration, and achievement are different kinds of experiences of "life and death". Many teachers and elders encourage with loving faces and tender words; many devotees make offering with respect and sincerity; many people commend with praise; many organizations reward with honors. They epitomize cultivation. Unless we emulate them, we cannot liberate ourselves from "numerous experiences of life and death".

I have been a monk for over sixty years. Some of my teachers and fellow monastics died young. Others died old. I have learned much from my "numerous experiences of life and death". Some Buddhists first approached the teachings after the death or injury of a family member, then offered their time and labor to society. Others who had a more affirmative reason for their practice and cultivation searched for meaning in their lives after realizing the illusory nature of worldly phenomena. The key to understanding lies in "numerous experiences of life and death".

Everyone experiences birth, aging, sickness, and death. Our minds experience formation, continuance, mutability, and extinction. Matter experiences formation, existence, destruction, and non-existence. There is nothing wrong with transmigration. It is perfectly natural, like the cells of the body renewing themselves. It's a pity that many people fear it, and live like walking corpses. Mencius said, "Before heaven confers on someone great responsibility it makes him suffer poverty." Ch'an teaches that, "To practice meditation, one must experience transformation." Remember also that, "However desperate your situation, springtime remains an enchanting vision." Life never dies. To move forward on our march to perfection, we must grasp the essential meaning of "numerous experiences of life and death".

Don't Be a Dolphin

When I first arrived in Taiwan I helped Venerable Miao Kuo with mail and official documents. He was in charge of Hsinchu subdivision of the Chinese Buddhist Association. Although he always kindly served me a glass of milk after my day's work, I was not pleased. I felt like a performing dolphin at Sea World who gets tossed a small fish. Many years later I cannot help remembering this when I see disciples of mine fishing for a reward or praise after finishing a job I have assigned. Then I say to them, "Don't be a dolphin for a small fish."

Since ancient times, we have considered dolphins the most intelligent of animals. At the same time, they have the greedy habits of animals. Men, as well, are intelligent and greedy. For that reason, leaders must motivate their subordinates with rewards. Emperors awarded victorious generals land and rank. Governors awarded benefactors medals or titles of nobility. To avert foreign aggression, emperors would establish peaceful relations through marriage. To subdue rebellion, emperors would address complaints. In Chinese history, for example, Yao married his daughter to Shun; Emperor Tai Chung married his

daughter Princess Wen Chen to a Tibetan king;
Kuang-yin Chao was crowned emperor and then
reduced the power of his officials. We can see from
this that mankind behaves like the dolphin who is
pleased with a small fish.

The mentality of the dolphin is destructive to
civilized society. Let anyone make even a trivial
contribution to society, and he expects to be
rewarded with a high position. Some people
demonstrate against the government just to gain
some small advantage. Some politicians take bribes
or conduct unethical election campaigns. What is
worse, some have put their country in grave
danger by spying for the enemy. Some countries
arm other countries to gain their support, leading
to international conflict. These examples show that
the mentality of the dolphin is detrimental to
morals and commerce. We must never forget that
such a state of mind leads to internal and
international chaos.

Since Sakyamuni Buddha discovered the
Dharma, many highly cultivated Chinese
monastics have wisely guided the Sangha by
instruction and not by reward. Without tossing a
fish, they have nurtured the disciples' life of
wisdom through the teachings of the Buddha.

Because of this, many people have aspired to practice Buddhism. For example, the Buddha practiced with compassion and justice, and was even willing to sacrifice his life. The elder Purna was ready to sacrifice his life for the Buddha. In China, Venerable Master Chien Chen[1] would have sacrificed his life for a larger purpose. Venerable Master Shen An developed his mind and resolve unceasingly. Their words and deeds aim to educate people, and are worthy of emulation. Unlike dolphins, people do not necessarily work for small fish. We should embrace the ideal of benefiting society without a thought of reward.

I was always moved when I read the lives of highly cultivated monastics. After arriving in Taiwan, I watched many people frolic like trained dolphins for some small personal advantage, without a thought for advancing Buddhism. "If I do not do it, who will?" My compassion and vow welled up in me. I worked hard to bring people together wherever I taught. I procured rooms,

---

[1] Master Chien Chen was the first Chinese monk to bring Buddhism to Japan. At the request of two Japanese monks, he attempted to sail there in 743 C.E. After five failures, he and his disciples finally arrived in 754 C.E., where he established a temple and conducted precepts ceremonies.

chairs and tables, and I printed fliers. I sought to make a mental offering for the multitude, but not of the mentality of a dolphin. From that time, Buddhism in Taiwan expanded rapidly. Those who took refuge forty years ago have continually supported Buddhism ever since. Such is the importance of Buddhist education.

For a long time, I wrote Buddhist articles for such magazines as *Life Monthly, Bodhi Tree, Buddhism Today,* for radio, and for newspapers. I never charged for them, and I paid for postage and transportation. I persisted because I was perfectly willing to do so. I remember that when I went to Taipei from Ilan to edit *Life Monthly*, the elder in charge always said during the meal, "See, we knew you were coming, and that's why we have prepared special dishes for you." Though he was sincere, I did not agree with his idea. I thought, "I'm obliged to work. Do I work hard just for a small reward?" It's important to appraise services rendered and repay them accordingly; but don't give out of the mentality of feeding a dolphin. A dolphin with moral courage wags its tail happily when the audience applauds. It does not perform just to gain a small fish. And what about us? It is our sacred business to propagate Buddhist teachings with written articles.

In 1959, I was appointed to the committee of the newly reorganized Chinese Buddhist Association. I was glad to do something for Buddhism in Taiwan. I worked hard and offered occasional suggestions. But I was disappointed to discover that the elders did not aim for reform. Though I was grateful to those elders who named me a standing director when I was not yet famous and could not even afford room and board, I would have been satisfied just to have a worktable. How could I, a young monk without merits and virtues, assume so high an honor? But I thought of K'o-fa Shih, during the Ming dynasty [1368-1644 C.E.], who would rather die protecting the town of Yangchou than be bribed by the rising Ch'ing dynasty [1644-1911 C.E.]. Ch'i-chao Liang returned a bribe of a hundred thousand silver dollars to Shih-kai Yuang, and persisted in publishing his article *Comments on the Nation's Affairs*. I was a disciple of the great Buddha, and an adherent of the Mahayana school. How could I behave like a dolphin at Sea World satisfied with a small fish? So I turned down the offer of standing director.

For fifty years, I lacked causes and conditions to attend any of the World Fellowship of Buddhists

(WFB) conferences. When I was young, I wished to serve as a representative, but was impeded by officials of the Chinese Buddhist Association. Even so, I was glad to assist the Association. Since then, with sufficient causes and conditions, I have helped organize three of the last twenty conferences. By hosting two of them outside Asia, I helped the WFB enter the international stage. The 16th conference was held at Hsi Lai Temple, Los Angeles, the 18th at Fo Guang Shan, Taiwan, and the 20th at Nan Tien Temple, Australia. I provided free room and board, transportation, and conference facilities.

At the 18th conference, I was recommended for honorary president. At the 20th, in 1998, I was asked to be president of the World Fellowship of Buddhists. I turned it down because I was busy with the affairs of Buddha's Light International Association. At any rate, there are plenty of international Buddhist leaders, such as His Holiness the Dalai Lama of Tibet, Venerable Thich Nhat Hanh of Vietnam, Venerable Dhammananda of Malaysia, Venerable Wol Ha of Korea, Mizutani Kousei of Japan, and Venerable Rajabhavanavisudh of the Dhammakaya Foundation, Thailand. They are the ones to lead the World Fellowship of Buddhists. Because they do not act like dolphins seeking small fish, they should not be fed with small fish, but with support and applause.

In 1954, I led the Ilan chanting group. We had to raise funds to build a lecture hall because we did not have a regular place to practice. Mr. Chang of Ilan County Hall said to me, "The mother of the president of the Taiwan Cement Company died. Please preside at her funeral service. They are willing to provide the cement for the hall." Unmoved, I replied, "What's great about cement? I wouldn't go there even if they built it with gold." Young and stubborn, I did not believe that everything could be solved with small fish. When a devotee died the next day, I chanted and prayed for him without being invited, and even accompanied his body to the cemetery. For that I received a red envelope with NT$60 from his family, which I donated to the *Buddhist Devotees' Newsletter.* The Dharma cannot be bought with small fish.

"A virtuous person gets money by proper means." Although we need clothing, food, and other things, just as the dolphin needs small fish, some things are more important. There is the precious friendship of practice and cultivation, shared ideas, and so forth. Above all, we cannot allow our dignity to be trampled.

Thirty years ago I performed Dharma functions for seven days with twelve disciples at a Buddhist Hall in Chiayi. In gratitude, the person in charge offered us a load of fabric, especially valuable in a time of shortage. Not only did I turn it down, I even paid for my disciples' visit to Mt. Ali to show them my gratitude. In my view, dolphins perform for small fish, but people should live for something better. For these many decades, no matter how busy we have been I have always sent my disciples to help out at other temples. What I cherish is better than small fish.

Once, while working on official documents in the Dharma Hall at Fo Guang Shan, I received a message from my attendant. A devotee was offering me NT$100,000 if I would go to the Ma-chu complex for it. I turned him down at once. A week later, when Tzu Hui told me that a devotee wanted to donate NT$200 to Fo Guang University, I was happy to meet with him. My attendant wondered why my attitude was so different. "Because the latter realizes the importance of education, and he doesn't treat me like a dolphin," I explained.

Several years ago, when Mr. Ti-wu Wang, founder of the *United Daily News*, passed away, I presided over a chanting service and prayed for him. Subsequently, his son, Bi-chen Wang, came with a red envelope with money. I told him, "To get along with others, money can show appreciation, affection can show appreciation, and righteousness can show appreciation. Isn't it better to go beyond money, affection, and righteousness to make affinity with Buddhism?" Mr. Wang, a wise man, realized my meaning instantly.

Sometimes I help my friends in education, culture, and the arts. I often help Buddhist organizations with manpower and money. When my disciples say, "Master is silly to feed others with small fish," I reply, "I am a human, not a dolphin." People should help others in need, and not just for something in return.

When I eat bread, I eat the crust first. When I chew sugar cane, I chew the tough parts first. To suffer first or enjoy first is up to you. As for giving and receiving, are you going to eat the fish or feed others with it? We don't have to snatch a fish nervously as we work, like dolphins. We can wait. In the past, the United States gave Taiwan many small fish (financial assistance). Some Taiwanese remained in the United States after finishing school and contributed much to its economic growth and technological advance. I established Hsi Lai

University in Los Angeles to facilitate a cultural exchange between East and West, and I hope I have contributed to humanistic thinking there. Isn't that getting a big fish in return?

A minister once invited my devotee's sick friend to pray with him in the hospital. Before long the minister invited him to join his faith. When the patient declined, the minister declared he would go to hell. It's a shame that religion was so degraded by this episode.

It's fine to give others a scrap of paper, a painting, a bit of happiness, praise, encouragement, comfort, or some hope and blessing. But don't turn it into a business transaction, with goods delivered and payment made. The "generosity without attachment" in Buddhism, the so-called "triple contemplation of the emptiness of substance",[2] teaches us the fullest meaning of the relationship between giver and taker. We are human, not dolphins at Sea World.

That is why, whenever I conduct refuge ceremony, I make clear to participants, "After taking refuge in Buddhism, you can change your mind and believe in other religion. It's like going to

[2] 1. of the unreality of the giver, 2. of the unreality of the receiver, 3. of the unreality of the given.

a new school. When some sectarians say non-believers will be punished by heaven and struck by lightening, they are trying to control people through the authority of God. Buddhism is quite different. To take refuge in Buddhism is to take refuge in oneself. Within one's true nature lies the Triple Gem of the Buddha, the Dharma, and the Sangha. Taking refuge in Buddhism helps us know ourselves, and find our true nature..." Inspired by my explanation, many have taken refuge. I think that is because I do not regard people as dolphins, to be seduced with small fish.

Consider this interesting dialogue from the Ch'an literature. Ch'an Master Chao-chou Tsung-shen once reproached Venerable Wen Yen for prostrating to the Buddha. "Is the Buddha there for you to prostrate?" Venerable Wen Yen replied, "It is good to pay respects to the Buddha." The master rejoined, "Non-attachment is better than doing something good." There is also a famous saying by Ch'an Master Huang-po Hsi-yun, "Don't crave something from the Buddha, the Dharma, and the Sangha." It doesn't mean we should not pay respects to the Triple Gem. It tells us that believing in Buddhism is not for fame and profit, but for practicing the truth of the Buddha. By admitting, "I am the Buddha," we can gain real benefit.

I have never done charity work out of the mentality of the dolphin. I tell those who come to me for charity, "In Buddhism, we say 'the giver and the taker are equal'. Thank you for giving us an opportunity to make affinity. I hope you bring home happiness and peace." I have never expected to get something in return for a bag of rice, a bottle of oil, an electric fan, or a cooker. In fact, I should repay those people for giving us the chance to practice generosity. Therefore, I pray sincerely for them. I hope the Buddhist teaching of equality helps people respect and tolerate one another. I hope my goodwill can be everywhere for everyone, so we may all enjoy happiness and world peace.

When Bodhidharma, the First Patriarch of Ch'an school in China, came to China by sea, Emperor Wu [464-549 C.E.] of the Liang dynasty asked, "I have built temples everywhere for monastics to practice and cultivate. What's the merit of it?" Bodhidharma reprimanded him, "No merit at all." Then he added, "Merit cannot be sought in this way." Merit with attachment is finite and limited, while the merit of non-attachment is infinite and limitless.

Concerning real generosity, the *Diamond Sutra*

says there should be no attachment of giver, taker, and the thing given. "Emptiness" does not mean nothing. "Emptiness" intermingles you and me, have and have-not. The concept "emptiness" makes our world spacious and averts binding us to small fish, as dolphins are.

Readers' Digest once described a dolphin named Fungi in Dingle, County Kerry, Ireland. Caring and understanding, he brought happiness to the local people, and helped cure their mental wounds. Usually, when a dolphin swims in a shallow place, he stays at most an hour. But Fungi stayed over thirteen years. Nobody knows why. I think he stayed because he did not perform for small fish.

According to the Buddhist scripture, before becoming the Buddha's attendant, Ananda asked elder Maudgalyayana to convey to him three conditions. First, he would not wear the Buddha's clothes, old or new. Second, if any devotee invited the Buddha home for an offering, he would not go along. Third, he would not meet with the Buddha when it was not proper. The Buddha gladly agreed and praised his virtue. Because Ananda said from the start that he did not serve the Buddha for small fish, he became the Buddha's longest serving attendant. Thus the Buddha's teachings, abundant as the ocean, flowed into his mind, making us their fortunate possessors.

There was a monk who cooked for sixty years at Tien-tung Temple in China. At an advanced age, he still dried mushrooms in the sun. The Japanese monks who learned Buddhist teachings there respected him very much. If the old monk had acted like a dolphin for small fish, he would not have made aspiration to cook so long.

Nowadays, youth have the impatient mentality of the dolphin. It is not easy to get small fish. So they tend to change jobs very often, which leads to failure. Shouldn't we remind ourselves not to act like dolphins?

It is said, "As a monastic, you need to sound the bell every day." Ch'an Master Fu-shan Fa-yuan was scolded and asked by his abbot to leave. Not discouraged, he collected alms to learn the Dharma. Because he was persistent, he was accepted by Ch'an Master Kuei Sheng and received the robe and the Dharma. Ch'an Master Hsueh Tou preferred to toil in a temple for three years than show a letter of recommendation from the scholar Tseng Kung that would have gained him better treatment. With the support of heavenly guardians he became abbot of Ts'ui-feng Temple. The great practice and cultivation show us that only when we get along and handle affairs without asking anything in return are we respected and successful.

Therefore, I would like to give everyone this advice. If you work for practical benefit, you won't persist in your ideal. Though obligations and rights should be balanced, shouldering obligations is not for mere show, like a dolphin performing, and paying attention to rights is not to be done only to gain a small fish. We should master the concepts of right and wrong, and of achieving great merits. We need to understand that the meaning of life is to enlarge life continually in the universe. To lead an energetic life, we need to have a great vision and not perform for small fish.

*Handle Difficult Tasks
with Ease*

Until the Buddhist scholar and author Yi-hsuan T'ang began teaching at Buddhist colleges, he was for many years the director of a military hospital. Because of our great differences, he often disparaged my opinions and style. Though praise and blame have never mattered to me, I was surprised and flattered when he cheerfully declared that I "handle difficult tasks with ease". Looking back on my words and actions, clearly my skill in the arts of getting along and handling affairs is summarized in the verse of Ch'an Master Hsiang-yen Chih-hsien, "Leave behind no trace of attachment no matter where you go." Another way to say this is, "The dust stays unmoved after being swept by the shadow of bamboo; no trace is left after the wild goose flies across a deep pool." Letting go of the past, I refuse to calculate gain or loss, or be attached or regretful. But Mr. T'ang justly praised me, when he said that I "handle difficult tasks with ease".

I remember vividly the hard labors I was obliged to perform for the temple upon my arrival in Taiwan: fetching water, lugging bundles, cart dragging, grocery shopping, and much more. Because the residents thought I was content with tough chores, they heaped upon me everything that was laborious. In truth, tugging the cart uphill left me exhausted and close to vomiting. But I felt such profound gratitude to the temple that, in toiling for the multitude to repay my obligation, I gained constantly renewed strength. Forty years ago, I edited a magazine for a Buddhist elder while writing for various newspapers and magazines. Noting my willingness to write without compensation, the elder thought writing came easily to me. Actually, I often had to rack my brain for fresh ideas. Before long, I was also in charge of distribution and mailing. Keen to propagate Buddhist teachings, I was perfectly willing to do anything and go anywhere. Trains and cars were my offices, where I prepared my lectures. I spoke everywhere joyfully and spontaneously. Devotees called me quick-witted, and said I "handled difficult tasks with ease". They were delighted with my teaching. But my first years of Dharma propagation were full of hard work. Each lecture cost me a day to prepare. Now over seventy, I feel tired and thirsty after a day of speaking. But when I see the faces of eager devotees, I forget the hardship and am content.

"If you want to give someone a hard time," it

has been said, "persuade him to start Buddhist colleges, edit magazines, and build temples." During decades devoted to educating, editing, and temple building, I confronted a host of impediments thrown up by society. The registration of Fu-shan Temple was delayed eight years because bureaucrats shirked their duty. The construction of Hsi Lai Temple was hampered by protests from non-Buddhists. There were many natural disasters as well, such as the typhoon that produced flooding and a landslide at Fo Guang Shan, and collapsed the walls behind Chi-le Temple. We also assumed the failed undertakings of others. In the case of Fu-kuo and Yuan-fu temples, we discovered that we had to pay their debts. Because of my aspiration and vow, it is not at all hard for me to handle difficult situations. I treasure friendship and like to make good affinity, so I was always perfectly willing to accept hardships. I was willing to follow causes and conditions to make affinity, so it was not hard for me to lead an extremely busy life. I was willing to shoulder responsibilities, so I didn't feel powerless when I owned nothing. In short, I was able to "handle difficult tasks with ease" because I was willing to do everything without complaint or regret.

"Emptiness" is the world's most majestic concept. Manjusri Bodhisattva regards "emptiness" as the gateway to non-duality. Ch'an Master Hui K'ai regarded "emptiness" as the central principle of the Ch'an school. Hui Neng, the Sixth Patriarch, subdued arrogant fellow monastics with "emptiness". Through "emptiness", Ch'an Master T'ao Shu was not intimidated by the supernatural powers of a Taoist master. Like them, I have employed "emptiness" to overcome obstacles. When the military ordered Shou-shan Temple torn down, claiming that it was too close to one of their bases, I paid a visit to the commander and succeeded in getting the order rescinded. Behind Fo Guang Shan lie some privately owned orchards. The most convenient access to them passes through our temple grounds. Formerly, we permitted the owners to drive through our grounds to reach their orchards, but the resulting noise and congestion disturbed the serenity of the temple and irritated the temple visitors. When I decided to close the grounds to through traffic, the orchard owners blocked our gate with their angry demonstrations, preventing anyone from coming in or going out. But in the face of our calm but unyielding resistance, the demonstrators finally tired and, couple of days later, gave up. The Kuan-yin Incident nearly turned a park in Taipei into a battlefield of politics and religion. When the Buddha's tooth came to Taiwan, some non-Buddhists tried to harass us. I coped serenely with the storm. I persuaded through reason, educated with sincerity, and subdued with compassion. I don't have a fixed approach, but always keep "emptiness" in my mind, like a bright mirror. That is how I generate the endless power that drives these peaceable tactics, overcoming all obstacles with ease.

Fifty years ago, when no monastic cared to stay in Ilan, I volunteered to go there. Many military families lived in Ilan. Of the devotees, some were old, some were in their prime, and some were quite young. Some devotees had been with the temple a long time, but hadn't learned the right teachings. Some who had received a Japanese militarist education were hot-tempered, though loyal. Conservative old devotees rejected the young and energetic. But I have gotten along harmoniously with devotees in Ilan for many years. I promoted true Buddhism there, making Ilan the cradle of Buddhism in Taiwan. The devotees I used to know still care about me, and stand ready to help. They devoted themselves to procuring land and constructing Fo Guang University, and they strived to assuage the misgivings of the citizens and government. To those who ask why my devotees say I "handle difficult tasks with ease", I reply that it is because I have experienced the suffering of old age, the wisdom of maturity, and the strength of youth.

After founding temples throughout the world, I deal easily with devotees of varying temperament. I show soldiers, merchants, women, children, the elderly, and the disabled how the Dharma addresses their specific concerns. I have organized meditation classes and chanting services for those who love practice and cultivation, Buddhism classes and study groups for those who seek wisdom, classes and writing clubs for those who love the arts, and charity groups for those who wish to offer their services. I lecture according to people's capacities and inclinations, so they may apply the teachings in their daily lives and bring their talents into full play. That is how I have revitalized Buddhism.

"Better to lead a troop of soldiers than an assembly of monastics," they say. While monastics, happily, are more detached from passion and pain, they are hard to motivate because they do not seek material rewards. It is far tougher to guide monastics than to supervise employees. I have more than a million devotees worldwide, and over a thousand monastic disciples. Even though my days are crammed with temple business and Dharma propagation, I must still deal with the monastics' emotional problems, illnesses, and requests for leave, and manage their study, practice and cultivation. In my seminars, when asked how I supervise so many disciples, I reply that I follow the *Vimalakirti-nirdesa Sutra*, "Purge disciples' defilements according to their inclinations." That is how we easily change defilement to enlightenment and ignorance to wisdom. I train my disciples with ease, even the recalcitrant ones, because I keep my finger on the pulse of society. I teach each disciple according to his character and inclinations, patiently correct his mistakes, and put up with immaturity.

When a disciple has a marriage problem, I teach him "to win love with love". I resolve conflicts in the entertainment industry with the tale of Dighayu.[1] To reconcile politicians, I advise them,

---

[1] Following the instructions of his murdered father, he did not seek revenge, but moved the murderer to return his land.

"Retreat a step to open a broader horizon." I console the dying with the notion that "death is like migration". Because I know how to manage difficult problems, it is easy for me to solve property disputes, problems of children's education, and the occasional confusion in the minds of Buddhists.

I have taken part in all kinds of activities, including Dharma propagation in Shah Alam Stadium and the vow-taking movement of the compassionate, each of which drew eighty thousand participants. Every year, I lecture thousands at the Dr. Sun Yat-sen Memorial Hall, Taipei, and the Hunghom Coliseum, Hong Kong. Every annual conference and board of directors' meeting of Buddha's Light International Association is attended by thousands of representatives and observers. Thousands visit the fund-raising fairs of Fo Guang University. I am often asked, "How are you able to organize so many activities and provide so much room and board?" I think the key point is that our monastics are well trained. We plan thoroughly and cooperate well. No matter how large the crowd, or how tight the schedule, we succeed in "handling difficult tasks with ease" and efficiency.

When I established the first Buddhist college, some devotees warned me, "You don't have sufficient financial resources. Nobody will dare associate with you, and you will fail." Some in the Buddhist community added, "You do not have the experience to make it work." As I was planning a temple for Dharma propagation in the United States, a monk laughed at me. "You don't speak English. How can you propagate Buddhist teachings there?" When I registered at the Ministry of Education to establish Fo Guang University, a bureaucrat teased me. "It costs too much money and sweat. You had better think twice." When, on our thirtieth anniversary, I announced that we were closing Fo Guang Shan to visitors, someone tried to dissuade me. "If you close the temple, it will be hard for monastics to survive on donations." It is true that experience, language, and money are prerequisites for Dharma propagation. But, these are not important to monastics. Buddhist teachings, firm faith, and right understanding are more important. With these, I have founded sixteen Buddhist colleges with ease. Among them, Ts'ung Lin Buddhist College has operated over thirty years without interruption. I have now established over one hundred branches on six continents, and the number is increasing. I have operated Hsi Lai University, in Los Angeles, for ten years. The first students of Nan Hua University will graduate in 1998. Their number is increasing, and the management of the University is getting better. There are frequent exchanges with overseas universities and other cultural and educational organizations. After closing our gate in May 1997, monastics have led a simple and humble life. We still have organized weekend retreats for practice and cultivation, providing room and board for over a thousand participants. In addition, we have organized meditation retreats, seven-day retreats for chanting the Buddha's name, short-term monastic retreats, seminars, and conferences. We have educated many in the past two years. It seems we have "handled difficult tasks with ease".

Here is a list of more than fifty "firsts" in the Buddhist community of Taiwan that are attributed to me: the first Buddhist choir, the first Dharma propagation on TV, the first Buddhist record, building the first Buddhist lecture hall, the first Dharma propagation in the national hall, the first deluxe edition of a Buddhist book, the first organization with devotees in uniform, the first devotees' seminar, the first children's class, the first

Sunday class, the first preschool educational center, the first bright lamp Dharma function, the first Dharma propagation using slide projector and projection machine, the Chinese Culture University's Indian Culture Research Institute approved by the Ministry of Education, the first Buddhist summer camp for college students, the first urban Buddhist college, the first mobile clinic, the first public library, the first hospital ward for the dying, the first devotees' service center, the first gratitude Dharma function, the first fair, the first Sangha Day celebration, the first temple in a high-rise building, the first alms collection around the island, the first international Buddhist examination, the first Dharma function with Ch'an, Pureland, and Tantric practice together, the first activity of returning to the era of the Buddha, the first Buddhist museum, the first ceremony of handing down the Dharma, the first short-term monastic retreat, the first Buddhist canon with new punctuation and paragraphs, the first *Fo Guang Buddhist Dictionary* receiving the Golden Cauldron Award, the first Dharma preaching to military academies and islands near Taiwan, the first pilgrimage to India with two hundred devotees, the first meeting with the Pope at the

Vatican in 1997, and others. Many say that I am lucky to own so many "firsts". But they are not to my sole credit. It is through teamwork that we "handle difficult tasks with ease".

I have struggled to overcome every kind of frustration. Forty years ago, when I wrote in plain language for ordinary people, some conservative members of the Buddhist community dissented. When I led Buddhist youth in propagating the Dharma, the conservative monastics opposed me. I was sharply criticized for organizing a Buddhist choir to promote Buddhism through lively music. Police confiscated my slide projector without cause. When I established temples in high-rise buildings for easy access to Buddhism, bureaucrats refused to register them because they lacked the normal temple roof, with its upward projection. When I recorded programs for Dharma propagation and signed a contract with a television station, the show was cancelled on the ground that a monk could not be shown on television. Police often interfered with us when we propagated the Dharma on the street. But none of these annoyances could defeat me, because I believe that "where there is Dharma, there is a way". No matter how hard the task, I have the confidence to "handle it with ease".

In the spirit of perseverance despite setbacks, I have expanded my overseas undertakings and achieved several breakthroughs. In 1986, when the adherents of esotericism and exotericism were lacking a channel of communication, I organized a Tantric and Sutric Buddhist Conference to enable representatives from these two traditions to reach a consensus. They continue to communicate. Though China and Taiwan became enemies in 1949, I brought a Dharma propagation group to China in 1989, where we paid our respects to my teachers, elders, and relatives. In 1988, when the World Fellowship of Buddhists conference was convened at Hsi Lai Temple, I organized a meeting of representatives from China and Taiwan. This unexpected event was greeted with applause and tears. Since ancient times, monastic institutions have been set apart from the laity, with few ties between them. In 1992, I launched the Buddha's Light International Association (B.L.I.A.) for lay people. B.L.I.A. is joined to the Fo Guang Shan monastic order like arms on a man or wings on a bird. This unity improves the effectiveness of Dharma propagation. The bhiksuni precepts of the Theravada tradition have been ignored for at least two hundred years on account of war, the domination of monks, and other causes. After several attempts, I arranged the international full ordination of over two hundred bhiksunis of the Mahayana and Theravada traditions, witnessed by twenty-six highly cultivated monastics of both traditions, at Bodhgaya, India in February 1998. During the event, the Tibetan lama Kunga revealed his intent to give me a Buddha's tooth, a relic that he had guarded a very long time. Asked why he would give the relic to me, when the world was full of outstanding practitioners, he gave an account of my life, and declared to the world, "Venerable Master Hsing Yun is of international importance, and we believe he will appropriately care for the Buddha's tooth." To "handle difficult tasks with ease" is not as easy as it seems. But being moved by the ideal of Dharma propagation, to the benefit of Buddhism and sentient beings, I prefer not to praise myself to the multitude.

Many eminent Buddhists of historical importance have "handled difficult tasks with ease". I am just a drop in the ocean. Society and the state supported the great Buddha when he favored the equality of the four castes. The Buddha transmitted the Dharma to every part of India, even those ruled by alien faiths. His teaching brought peace to a warring land. Even in awkward circumstances, he could skillfully subdue the recalcitrant. His incomparable "handling difficult tasks with ease" has become the spiritual treasure of millions of Buddhists for over twenty-five hundred years.

Venerable Master T'ai Hsu, in a time of chaos, saved his country by exposing the evils of militarists. At a time when Buddhism was declining, he founded a vitally important journal, condemned injustice, proposed the reformation of the Sangha, and contended with the government to defend Buddhism. He studied the various Theravada traditions, and advocated teaching the core principles of the eight Mahayana schools. He had a first-rate knowledge of the world and of the Buddhist teachings. He wrote Buddhist history and commentaries on the teachings. When government officials proposed that temples be appropriated for educational purposes, he argued the Buddhist side without a thought for his safety. He was not discouraged when conservative monks united to attack him, but continued training monastics while promoting Buddhism worldwide. Buddhism survived the early years of the Republic because Venerable Master T'ai Hsu "handled difficult tasks with ease".

I will conclude with a few more examples.
Kasyapa-matanga subdued non-Buddhists with a
verse of righteousness, and laid a firm foundation
for Buddhism in China. Dharmodgata went to
western Gansu, China, to seek the Dharma at the
risk of his life. Venerable Fa Hsien sailed to India,
and Venerable Master Hsuan Tsang crossed vast
deserts to bring sutras from India. Ch'an Master Fa
Yen rebuffed the emperor with a verse. Venerable
Master Hui Yuan wrote *Monastics Should Not
Succumb to the Emperor*. Jen-shan Yang set up a
place in Nanjing to carve sutras. All of these
champions seem to "handle difficult tasks with
ease", but they actually had to endure a great
amount of stress. How admirable are their
compassion, wisdom, diligence, and courage.

These examples teach us that the secret of
"handling difficult tasks with ease" is mental
conviction. As long as you believe you can do them,
you will have the strength to "handle difficult tasks
with ease". Then you will be like flowing water,
carrying everything off without obstruction. The
key to "handling difficult tasks with ease" lies not
in avoiding difficulties and acting impulsively, but
in marrying wisdom with responsibility. Then we

can cultivate the ability to "handle difficult tasks with ease". Then we can demolish impediments as the Buddha did.

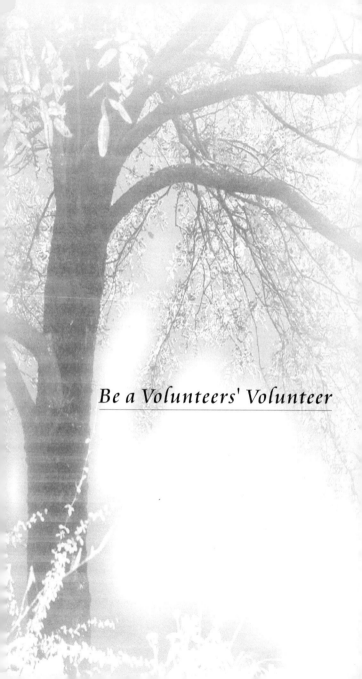

Be a Volunteers' Volunteer

Someone asked me, "Why does everyone love to work for you?"

I think the reason many volunteers work for me is that I never arrogantly give orders but always act as a "volunteers' volunteer".

In traditional society, people were classified as intellectuals, farmers, workers, and merchants. Nowadays, we have "office workers", "punks", "snails without shell",[1] and others. Since ancient times, one group has served the public and benefited society greatly while being almost forgotten. These are the "volunteers". Working without pay, their work is precious beyond measure. Working in silence, their joy is boundless. We treasure them because they work without prospect of reward. It is my ardent wish to serve these wonderful people as a "volunteers' volunteer".

Whenever I have asked volunteers to compose some sayings or a flier, I always prepared paper and ink and a space to work. When I have asked volunteers to plant grass or to water, I always fetched the bucket and hose and conducted them

---

[1] Those who cannot afford to buy their own houses.

to the faucet and toolbox. I prepared tea and snacks for them and invited them to dine with us. When they were ready to go home, I consoled them for their hard labor and thanked them for their achievements. I would not call it a day until I saw them pass from view.

Forty years ago, I invited Mr. Hsi-ming Yang, a military officer, to make drawings for Tzu-ai Kindergarten, which I founded. Before he arrived I prepared his brushes and paint. While he drew, I prepared his tea and noodles. When he volunteered to work with the kids, I served him as a volunteer, as if I were his apprentice. I served him any time he needed me. Afterwards, he took refuge in the Triple Gem.

At that time, Mr. Chia-chun Chu, the best art designer in Taiwan, was editing the *Young Lions* for the Salvation Corps. His designs were inventive and his headings attractive. While helping me edit *Awakening the World* and *Buddhism Today,* he always found upon arrival that paste, scissors, draft paper, and other stationery had been placed at the side of his desk. He also found a bed ready for him, with pillowcase and sheets freshly laundered and ironed. Though I was the Master, when he worked I was his attendant awaiting instructions. Come the cold midnight, I would prepare hot milk and snacks to quell his hunger. Working for me and at the same time editing the *Young Lions,* his fame increased. Through him I came to know many famous writers, including Shih-feng Kuo, Hai-ying Lin, Fan Ho, Hsuan Ya, Hsin Mei, and Kung-Sun Yen. It was a pity that he died young, for with his outstanding talent he could have contributed much to Buddhism.

Twenty years ago, when Chuan-huang Chiu headed the Social Workers' Association of the KMT party, he decided to ask Pei-keng Chang to serve as secretary-general of the Chinese Buddhist Association. Though I supported his choice, the conservatives rejected it. Subsequently, I invited Mr. Chang to be secretary-general of Fo Guang Shan. Because I served him like a page, fetching pen and paper, he was glad to work for me.

Thirty years ago, when I established the Buddhist Culture Service Center, I invited Ms. Hsin-tao Lee to run it. Every three to five days I would go there to help write letters or handle general affairs. Subsequently, she entered into monasticism with me, and was renamed Tzu Chuang. She has helped plan and build our overseas temples.

I am a competent art designer and magazine editor, and I can handle secretarial matters, such as planning and writing official letters. But more important, as a volunteers' volunteer I could inculcate Buddhist ideals and train people to serve the Buddhist community. When everything was on the right track, I could go elsewhere to propagate Buddhist teachings.

When the Buddha instructed his disciples to make food offerings to Hariti[2] and her children, she became a Buddhist guardian. Thanks to the teachings of Venerable Master Chih Yi,[3] Yun-chang Kuan[4] vowed to protect temples in future lifetimes. As "volunteers' volunteers", we must serve the volunteers and care about their needs above all. Several decades ago, when Sung-shan Weng was a painter's apprentice in Ilan, I invited him to carve Buddha's statues. I went often to his workplace to

---

[2] Hariti, kuei-zu-mu (Mother of Demon Children) in Chinese, had vowed to devour all the babies of the city of Rajagrha. The Buddha taught her a lesson in motherhood by hiding one of her five hundred children, giving her a taste of the heart-breaking pain that she had inflicted on other parents. Ultimately, she was converted and became a protector of the Dharma. Different versions of her story exist.

[3] [538-597 C.E.]. Founder of T'ien-t'ai school in China.

[4] A folk deity or guardian of temples.

make suggestions and give him art books. And I paid for his round trip ticket to Europe, where I served as his guide to the arts. He is now a prominent artist, with many magnificent Buddha's statues to his credit.

Though Ah Chiao was eager to serve the Buddhist community, she had to make a living for her poor family. After I solved her financial problems, she applied to be a *shih-ku*, a resident lay female practitioner, and has made aspiration to cook for the multitude.

Yung Chun preferred to be my driver, rather than director of the Pilgrims' Lodge. She drove me north and south, day or night. When others fell asleep, I would chat to keep her awake, though I myself was sleepy. We passed many years of conversation. To help my Dharma propagation, she has driven millions of miles. After constantly hearing my teachings and opinions, she became a fine director of the personnel department before she was thirty.

I assign jobs to my disciples after I have assessed their abilities and backgrounds. I also make sure their health allows them to do their work, and I see that they have enough food and clothing. There is a saying in the military, "To lead your troops, you must first win their hearts." To win people's hearts, you must be a volunteer for them. The best way to show gratitude to volunteers is to solve their problems, care about them, and respect them from the bottom of your heart. Do not rely on petty expressions of concern or some trifling gift. When you treat your volunteers justly, the mutual good affinity can last a very long time.

I generally come across as intelligent and sociable, adept at human relationships and affairs. The truth is, I was born awkward. The only merit I have had since childhood is that I love to be a "volunteer". Of all my brothers and sisters, I was the most willing to do household chores. Compared with other kids of my age, I was the most willing to influence others to do good. From my volunteer work, I have made precious friendships and learned basic work practices. After becoming a monk, I aspired to perform such menial tasks as cleaning the Buddha Hall, fetching water, cooking, and serving. I sought to sound the bell so agreeably that its sound would benefit sentient beings alive and dead. To improve my usefulness in the dining hall, I tried to figure out efficient ways to serve the multitude. I endeavored to cook delicious dishes despite limited resources. I wrote articles for the benefit of others. At Chiao-shan Buddhist College, as a student of nineteen, I proposed an exhibition of Buddhist cultural objects. I helped with the details of planning and advertising. Thousands of visitors attended. When it closed, I realized that the real prize for aspiring to work was wisdom and experience. The reward of a "volunteer", affinity and happiness, is beyond measure.

Shortly after arriving in Taiwan, I settled in Chungli. I rose early every morning and dragged my cart down the long dirt road to market. I woke sleepy peddlers to buy the daily necessities for eighty people at the temple. After breakfast, I cleaned the area quickly and then drew six hundred buckets of water from a well for the temple's residents. Since there was a shortage of utensils, I usually cleaned the restrooms with my hands. Whenever a resident passed away, I helped place the body in a wooden box and carry it to cremation. At harvest, I collected the temple's share of the rice grown by the farmers who rented the temple's fields. For that task, I wore clogs and bore a carrying pole on my shoulders. Despite a heavy workload at twenty-three, I was happy for my aspiration. Though there was jealous gossip, I was thankful to the abbot for allowing me to stay and work, so that I might cultivate my ability. The so-called "volunteer" may seem to work for others, but he retains the best part of the harvest.

Dravya, one of the Buddha's disciples, performed decades of hard work while serving guests sincerely as a receptionist. Even when a late visitor knocked at the door, he was happy to lead him by lantern to the guesthouse. Eventually his fingers came to radiate light, and he no longer needed the lantern. I am ashamed that my merits and virtues are not yet perfect, and that none of my limbs radiates light. When I serve others, however, my heart is glowing, because I am full of the Dharma joy. I think that is the greatest fortune in my life.

The ancient sage said, "To be dragon or elephant (to be outstanding) in the Buddhist community, begin with serving others." There is another saying, "Make affinity with others before attaining Buddhahood." In Buddhism, we do not focus on secular knowledge and eloquence, but on the enlightenment mind. From Buddhist scriptures, we know that many highly cultivated monastics practiced selflessness and became enlightened while working. For example:

Ch'an Master Hsueh Feng was in charge of cooking under Ch'an Master Tung Shan,

Ch'an Master Ching Chu was in charge of supplying rice under Ch'an Master Kuei Shan,

Ch'an Master Tao Kuang was in charge of supplying buckets under Ch'an Master Chao Ching,

Ch'an Master Kuang Hsi was in charge of gardening under Ch'an Master Mo Shan,

Ch'an Master Chih Tung was in charge of general affairs under Ch'an Master Tung Shan,

Ch'an Master Hsiao Ts'ung was in charge of supplying lamps under Ch'an Master Yun Chu,

Ch'an Master Chi Shan was in charge of supplying logs under Ch'an Master To Tze, and

Ch'an Master Yi Huai was in charge of cleaning toilets under Ch'an Master Ts'ui Feng.

In addition, Ch'an Master Shih Shuang sifted rice, Ch'an Master Yun Yen made shoes, Ch'an Master Lin Chi planted pines, Ch'an Master Yang Shan herded cows, Ch'an Master Tung Shan planted tea, Ch'an Master Yun Men carried rice, Ch'an Master Hsuan Sha chopped wood, Ch'an Master Chao Chou swept grounds, Ch'an Master Tan Hsia weeded, Ch'an Master Lan Jung cooked, Venerable Master Yin Kuang served in the dining hall, and there are many other examples. They tell us that the meaning of work lies in expanding ourselves, serving the multitude, and enhancing the value of life. What can compare to the work of volunteers?

I lack the deep wisdom of the ancient sages. But in dedicating myself to working, I have realized the many ways to get along and handle affairs, and have vowed to teach my precious experiences to those who are willing to serve. When I was the president of the Buddhist college, I explained to the students beforehand the types of chores they must perform, their importance, and how to perform them. That enabled them to realize the Buddhist teachings as they worked, and to be efficient in their learning and practice. Whenever I organized an activity at Fo Guang Shan, I first held a seminar for the volunteers to tell them what to do, and when it was over we met to discuss the results. In that way, they could learn, enhance their work skills, and be filled with the Dharma joy.

These good causes and conditions have attracted many devotees. Some serve well at home, volunteering at Fo Guang Shan whenever there are activities. Some have flown ten hours across the Pacific, at their own expense, to serve at Hsi Lai

Temple. Some don an apron and roll up their sleeves to serve in the dining hall or help in the kitchen. Their aspiration and sincerity are equal to those of Emperor Wu [464-549 C.E.] of the Liang dynasty, who three times served in Tung-t'ai Temple. The admirable Emperor Hsuan, of the Western Han dynasty [206 B.C.E.-8 C.E.], when he was a prince served in a temple. No job is superior or inferior. As long as one is willing to serve, one can enjoy happiness and freedom. No job is easy or hard. As long as one is willing, one can do a trifling job well, or execute a complex undertaking splendidly.

Though Sakyamuni Buddha has entered into nirvana, his Dharmakaya is omnipresent. A volunteer of this world, he even now educates sentient beings with his supernatural powers. Avalokitesvara Bodhisattva, a volunteer of the suffering sea, responds to the calls of suffering beings. Ksitigarbha Bodhisattva, a volunteer of the tormenting hell, has been acclaimed for his great vow, that, "He would not attain Buddhahood unless the hell becomes empty". An ecological volunteer of the pureland, Amitabha Buddha beautifies his pureland with the lotus pond of seven treasures, the water of eight merits, roads paved with gold, and avenues of trees. Because the Buddhas and Bodhisattvas perform Buddhist undertakings diligently, they bring light to the dark world. We ordinary beings lack their virtue and means. But how can we be so lazy, so devoted only to our own little lives? Buddhist volunteers should not serve the Triple Gem only, but must also emulate the untiring spirit of the Buddhas and Bodhisattvas, bringing happiness to all sentient beings.

Based on this ideal, I established Buddha's Light International Association in 1992, and have advised all chapter and subchapter officers and members to organize all kinds of activities to benefit society and purify people's minds. We have cooperated and achieved greatly in these years and won recognition from the multitude. For example, the "caring mothers" who escort students safely across streets have won praise from many parents. Volunteers have helped many aged patients register in hospitals. The friendly service team has helped many poor families. The study groups have motivated many families to create the right atmosphere for study. In addition, there are tree plantings to save water, the seven precepts movement to purify people's minds, performances by the mentally retarded, environmental actions to save used paper, help for drug addicts, and more. With the enthusiastic support of B.L.I.A. members and volunteers, all these activities have been successful. In 1996, the international Buddhist examination, organized by the Fo Guang Shan Foundation for Culture and Education, attracted a million participants and over thirty thousand volunteer helpers. All these activities are a refreshing fountain to a society thirsty for moral regeneration.

I have received letters from all over the world recently, some praising the benevolent work of B.L.I.A., others inviting B.L.I.A. to co-sponsor activities for the public interest. I would do anything, great or small, to benefit the public; therefore, I never turn people down. I don't think I deserve praise. We are just volunteers connecting people with all good causes and conditions, doing what we must to create a pureland on earth.

Some devotees with a successful career often say to me that they would like to volunteer to serve the multitude when they retire. To be a volunteer, you don't have to wait until tomorrow. Right here and now you can carry out the spirit of a volunteer, the way of the Bodhisattva, to benefit sentient beings with four embracing virtues[5] and six perfections.[6] If you are willing to serve, you don't have to wait until you retire. You can do it now, and be a Bodhisattva of non-regressing and non-rest. It is a rare thing to be born human, but it is hard to seize this rare chance to have good causes and conditions. We must grasp every minute, every second, to make good affinity with others, to make our lives matter.

---

[5] Generosity, caring words, altruistic conduct, and working with and for others.
[6] Generosity, moral conduct, patience, effort, concentration, and wisdom.

Hsing Yun's Hundred Sayings Series

A drop of water is minute and feeble. But when many drops come together, they can become a stream that breaks rocks. If we have firm belief, we can easily adapt to any situation, doing everything with a happy mind and in a state of equanimity. Firm belief always finds a way. The Dharma lives among us. With it, we can live happily. This is why Master Hsing Yun emphasized, "Where there is Dharma, there is a way."

在煩惱交煎的人生苦海裡，擁有真實的「佛法」，能令一個人忍勞耐怨的增益己所不能，從而不斷地超越自己，實現生命的真義。有了佛法，生活在世間才能擁有美滿的人生。如何應用佛法於生活中，本套書將給您開闊性的引導。

Perfectly Willing
心甘情願

Publisher:Hsi Lai University Press
156pp., 4.5*7.13,paper
ISBN 0-9642612-0-0
US$6.95

Happily Ever After
皆大歡喜

Publisher:Hsi Lai University Press
152pp., 4.5*7.13,paper
ISBN 0-9642612-1-9
US$6.95

The Philosophy of Being Second
老二哲學

Publisher:Hsi Lai University Press
180pp., 4.5*7.13,paper
ISBN 0-9642612-7-8
US$6.95

Where There Is Dharma There Is a Way
有佛法就有辦法

Publisher:Fo Guang Cultural Enterprise Co.,Ltd.
186pp., 4.5*7.13,paper
ISBN957-543-968-6
US$6.95

Foguang Cultural Enterprise Co., Ltd.
117 Sec. 3 San He Rd., Sanchung, Taipei County, Taiwan, R. O. C.
E-mail:fgce@ms25.hinet.net
TEL:886-2-29800260   FAX:886-2-29883534
Buddha's lighr publishing
3456 S. Glenmark Drive, Hacienda Heights, CA. 91745, U.S.A.
E-mail:itc@blia.org   TEL:1(626)9619697   FAX:1(626)3691944

Sakyamuni's one hundred fables in comic series

1－20冊

百 喻 經 圖 畫 書

Children literature scholars and pictorial artists used simple text and picturesque presentation to illustrate the famous Buddhist fables. The series are in 20volumes with 40stories.
This series has received an award from the government for Oustanding vocational book for senior and junior high schools.

本套書為第一套佛教寓言圖畫書，由國內兒童文學家、插畫家共同將《百喻經》以生動的文字和圖畫方式呈現，篇篇精采動人。全書共二十冊、四十則故事，獲行政院新聞局第十四次優良中小學課外讀物推介。

Publisher:Fo Guang Cultural Enterprise Co.,Ltd.
NT$3000

Foguang Cultural Enterprise Co., Ltd.
117 Sec. 3 San He Rd., Sanchung, Taipei County, Taiwan, R. O. C.
E-mail:fgce@ms25.hinet.net
TEL:886-2-29800260   FAX:886-2-29883534